International Risk Management

Edited By

Margaret Woods, Peter Kajüter and Philip Linsley

ELSEVIER

AMSTERDAM • BOSTON • HEIDELBERG • LONDON
NEW YORK • OXFORD • PARIS • SAN DIEGO
SAN FRANCISCO • SINGAPORE • SYDNEY • TOKYO
CIMA Publishing is an imprint of Elsevier

CIMA

PUBLISHING

CIMA Publishing is an imprint of Elsevier
Linacre House, Jordan Hill, Oxford OX2 8DP, UK
30 Corporate Drive, Suite 400, Burlington, MA 01803, USA

First edition 2008

British Library Cataloguing in Publication Data
A catalogue record for this book is available from the British Library

978 0 7506 85658

For information on all CIMA publications
visit our website at www.cimapublishing.com

Typeset by Integra Software Services Pvt. Ltd, Pondicherry, India
www.integra-india.com

Printed and bound in Great Britain
08   09   10   10 9 8 7 6 5 4 3 2 1

International Risk Management

Contents

Preface

This book is the product of several years of debate amongst a number of risk researchers from across Europe on the problems of risk management and the associated accounting issues. The growth in popularity of Enterprise Risk Management (ERM) serves to highlight the complexity of risk management and its breadth as a discipline. There are numerous approaches to categorising risks under a series of different headings, and they straddle amongst other things like legal, economic, financial, human resource management and political issues. The result is that it is difficult to define the boundaries of risk management. The subject is made even more complex because of variations in risk management practice and governance regulations around the world.

The aim of this book is to draw attention to issues that are currently the subject of debate within three core dimensions of risk management: Risk Management Systems, Risk and Governance and Risk and Accounting. The first Part of the book, co-authored by German, Italian and UK-based writers, begins with a review of international regulations on risk management and internal control by Kajüter, Linsley and Woods. The review includes a comparison of risk management and internal control practices in different corporate governance systems, namely the single board and the two-tier board structure that exists in the UK and Germany. Following this analysis, Woods provides a detailed critique of the COSO Framework for internal control, which has become integrated into the legislative requirements of the Sarbanes–Oxley Act 2002, and the final chapter of the Part A is a detailed case study by Beretta and Bozzolan of risk management practice in Telecom Italia. The case outlines how the company installed a system based upon the COSO Framework and it details the problems and lessons learned throughout this process.

Part B of the book addresses the overlap between risk and governance issues. There are multiple parties who carry some responsibility for risk management within an organisation and this Part looks in depth at the role played by three parties. Berry looks at risk management through the lens of a non-executive director, because current regulatory thinking has given these directors a pivotal role in ensuring the existence of effective internal controls. The governance responsibilities and risk management issues for company directors who operate a pension fund are covered in the chapter by Chris O'Brien. The last chapter in this Part by Woods and Humphrey considers the role to be played by both internal and external auditors in relation to risk management, and the implications of changing trends in risk management for the audit profession.

Part C of the book recognises the potentially important risk management role to be played by both management and financial accountants and also corporate treasurers. Collier and Berry report on the extent to which management accountants are involved in risk-related activities on a day-to-day basis. Helliar focuses on the tools available and current practice in the management of interest rate risk which is generally seen as a Treasury-based task. Linsley, Shrives and Kajüter comment on risk disclosures in annual reports. The chapter covers both the theoretical origins of risk reporting and an international comparison of risk disclosure requirements and practice.

The co-editors hope that you will find the book both useful and thought-provoking, and would appreciate any comments on its content.

Margaret Woods, Nottingham University Business School
Peter Kajüter, University of Münster
Philip Linsley, University of York

List of Contributors

Sergio Beretta, Bocconi University, Italy
Anthony J. Berry, Manchester Metropolitan University, UK
Saverio Bozzolan, University of Padova, Italy
Paul M. Collier, Monash University, Australia
Christine Helliar, University of Dundee, UK
Christopher Humphrey, Manchester Business School, UK
Peter Kajüter, University of Münster, Germany
Philip Linsley, University of York, UK
Chris O'Brien, Nottingham University Business School, UK
Philip Shrives, Northumbria University, UK
Margaret Woods, Nottingham University Business School, UK

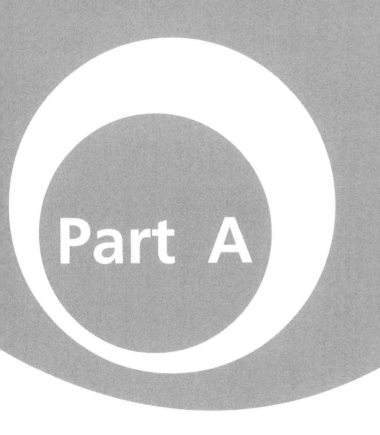

Part A

Risk Management Systems

Risk Management, Internal Control and
Corporate Governance: International Perspectives

Peter Kajüter*, Philip Linsley† and Margaret Woods‡

*University of Münster, Germany
†University of York, UK
‡Nottingham University Business School, UK

Introduction

Prominent corporate failures and bankruptcies such as Enron, Ahold, Parmalat and Philipp Holzmann have occurred in almost all industrial countries in the past decade and have led to an increasing interest in risk management in both academia and practice. The discussion of risk issues has been fuelled by regulatory initiatives that have been launched in many countries to specify the requirements for corporate governance, internal control and risk management in response to these corporate crises and scandals. Furthermore, professional organisations have developed frameworks for managing business risk. For example, the Association of Insurance and Risk Managers published a risk management standard in 2002 and COSO published the Enterprise Risk Management (ERM) Framework in 2004.

Despite similar objectives, the regulatory initiatives in the major industrial countries differ as regards their scope and degree of binding. Such differences in the risk management regulation are of relevance for several reasons. First, subsidiaries of international groups may have to comply with different national regulations which have to be considered when establishing a group-wide risk management system. Second, national regulations may impact on companies of other countries if they are obliged to comply with these regulations due to a listing in that country. The Sarbanes–Oxley Act (SOX) of the United States is an example in this respect. Third, national risk management regulations may influence the further development of regulatory requirements in other countries by a process of international harmonisation.

The objective of this chapter is, therefore, to analyse the current norms of risk management in major industrial countries of different legal and cultural regions. The analysis includes Germany, the UK, USA, Australia and Japan and is confined to general rules and regulations that are mandatory or recommended across sectors; industry-specific norms that exist for the banking and insurance industry, for instance, are not considered. In addition to this international comparison, the German and British risk management norms are analysed in more detail from the perspective of corporate governance and internal control. As a basis for the analysis the following section outlines the theoretical foundations that underpin the implementation of risk management systems.

Economic foundations of corporate risk management and risk management regulation

Corporate risk management

Capital market theory suggests that there is no need for corporate risk management in efficient capital markets because investors are able to manage the risks themselves. They can eliminate unsystematic risk by diversification and can transfer systematic risk to third parties by derivatives. As a consequence, risk management on the corporate level is irrelevant and actually reduces shareholder value due to its costs. This conclusion, however, is based on the narrow assumptions of the capital market theory (for example, rational investors, symmetric information and absence of transaction costs). If these assumptions are modified and market imperfections introduced, several reasons for corporate risk management emerge (Stulz, 1996; Tufano, 1998; Doherty, 2000).

Market imperfections are a key premise of agency theory (Ross, 1973; Jensen and Meckling, 1976; Fama, 1980). This theory assumes that information asymmetries and conflicts of interest are present between principals (shareholders) and agents (directors). As a result the management of a firm is usually better able to identify and assess business risks than the investor. Corporate risk management thus facilitates exploitation of a comparative advantage that resides with the management. Moreover, a risk management system can be perceived as a means of mitigating the information and incentive problems within a firm. It can act as a monitoring mechanism that reduces the information asymmetry between the management board and subordinate managers and contributes to the avoidance of opportunistic behaviour by the latter.

Finally, contingency theory argues that there is no 'one best' solution for corporate risk management. The design and effectiveness of management control systems in general, and risk management systems in particular, depend on a number of internal and external context factors (Waterhouse and Tiessen, 1978; Otley, 1980). Firm size, organisational structure and industry are examples of internal context factors, whereas dynamics and complexity of the environment are examples of external context factors that have been observed to influence the design of management control systems (Chenhall, 2003). Contingency theory thus helps explain the large variety of risk management systems in practice.

Risk management regulation

If corporate risk management can be explained solely from an economic point of view as outlined above, then regulation should be unnecessary. Risk management regulation reduces flexibility and causes costs for both the firm (ensuring compliance) and the public (monitoring compliance). However, normative regulation theory justifies regulatory initiatives on the grounds of losses in social welfare, market failure and the need to protect specific stakeholders (e.g. Ugochukwu Uche, 2001). Such arguments can be applied to risk management regulation as it is conceivable that risks may not be handled adequately due to information asymmetries and conflicts of interest. Ineffective risk handling may eventually result in a corporate crisis which in turn causes a series of corporate failures and bankruptcies at other firms, finally leading to significant losses in social welfare. Furthermore, public trust in capital markets might be damaged and investors might experience losses. Regulation is supposed to improve the efficiency of capital markets in this case. The actual economic benefit of risk management regulation remains an open question, though, because its potential advantages cannot be quantified in practice.

As the economic benefit of risk management regulation cannot be determined, it is also impossible to evaluate the benefit of alternative forms of regulation. The following section therefore reviews different national regulations of risk management without assessing their relative preference.

Regulatory requirements of risk management: An international comparison

Risk management regulation in major industrial countries

An international review of the regulatory requirements for risk management reveals that in most countries norms for risk management can be found in several legal sources. In general, there are two regulatory approaches for risk management.

- *Legislation*. In this case legislators establish binding rules for risk management and enforce them by imposing sanctions on those firms which do not comply with the rules. The rules are set either directly by law or indirectly via directives of regulatory bodies with legislative power (e.g. stock exchange supervisory authorities). Examples of this type of risk management regulation are § 91 par. 2 AktG (Stock Corporation Act) in Germany or §§ 302 and 404 of the SOX and the corresponding SEC-Releases in the United States.

- *Soft law*. In this case private standard setters develop rules for risk management as part of corporate governance codes. These rules are recommendations but entail an implicit pressure to comply, where firms have to publish a statement of compliance ('comply-or-explain'). Examples of this type of regulation can be found in many countries, for example in the German Corporate Governance Code, the British Combined Code or the Australian Principles of Good Governance and Best Practice Recommendations (Government Commission German Corporate Governance Code, 2006; Financial Reporting Council, 2006; ASX Corporate Governance Council, 2003).

In addition, there are a number of non-binding standards that have been developed by professional institutes or national standard setters, such as the (revised) Turnbull Report in the United Kingdom (Financial Reporting Council, 2005a), the COSO Enterprise Risk Management Framework in the United States (COSO, 2004), the Guide to Compliance with ASX Principle 7: 'Recognize and Manage Risks' in Australia (Group of 100, 2003) or the 'Guidelines for Internal Control that Functions Together with Risk Management' in Japan (METI Study Group, 2003). The aim of these standards is to provide guidance for implementing corporate risk management in firms. Compared to the legislation or soft law, these standards are usually much more concrete. In some cases, legal rules refer to these standards for further details. However, as these standards are recommendations, there are no sanctions in the case of non-adoption.

Table 1.1 provides an overview of the various sources of risk management regulation in Germany, the UK, USA, Australia and Japan. In addition, there are professional pronouncements issued by the external and internal auditing bodies (e.g. IDW PS 340 and IIR Revisionsstandard Nr. 2 in Germany, the Position Statement 'The Role of Internal Audit in Enterprise-wide Risk Management' of the Institute of Internal Auditors in the United States) which are not included in Table 1.1 as they are focused on auditing issues. The comparison in Table 1.1 shows that the national approaches to risk management regulation reflect the country's legal tradition. In Germany and Japan, for instance, the regulatory requirements for risk management are primarily codified in the company law while 'soft law' combined with control by capital markets dominates in the Anglo-Saxon countries. The SOX is a remarkable exception in this respect

Table 1.1 Risk management regulations

	Germany	UK	USA	Australia	Japan
Laws	§ 91 par. 2 AktG (1998)	–	§§ 302 and 404 Sarbanes-Oxley Act (2002)	–	§§ 21–7 Special Exceptions Law for the Commercial Code; § 193 Enforcement Regulation for the Commercial Code (2003)
Directives of Stock Exchange Supervisory Authorities	–	–	SEC-Release No. 33-8124 and No. 33-8238	–	–
Corporate Governance Codes	German Corporate Governance Code (revised 2006)	The Combined Code on Corporate Governance (revised 2006)	Final NYSE Corporate Governance Rules (2003)	Principles of Good Corporate Governance and Best Practice Recommendations (2003)	Revised Corporate Governance Principles (2001) Principles of Corporate Governance for Listed Companies (2004)
Standards and other Pronouncements	–	Turnbull Report: Internal Control (revised 2005)	COSO: Internal Control – Integrated Framework (1992) COSO: Enterprise Risk Management – Integrated Framework (2004)	AS/NZS 4360:2004 Risk Management (2004) Group of 100: Guide to Compliance with ASX Principle 7 (2003) ASX CG Council: Guidance in relation to the interpretation of Principle 7 (2003)	JIS Q 2001: Guidelines for development and implementation of risk management system (2001) METI Study Group: Guidelines for Internal Control that Functions Together with Risk Management (2003)

because it defines binding rules that are, however, part of the capital market law. This applies also for the SEC-Releases.

A closer look at the corporate governance codes in the five countries reveals differences in the extent to which risk management rules are considered. In the Australian Principles of Good Corporate Governance, for example, the risk management rules form a self-contained section of the code. They have, thereby, a prominent position within the various other rules of the code. In the German Corporate Governance Code, on the contrary, the rules are integrated in different parts of the code. The British Combined Code contains only a general requirement to establish an internal control system (which includes a risk management system). Furthermore, the rules regarding compliance with the codes differ. While the New York Stock Exchange Corporate Governance rules are mandatory for all companies listed on this stock exchange, the 'comply-or-explain' principle is used in Germany, the UK and Australia. No statement of compliance is required in Japan, however.

Comparison of objectives, scope and content of national risk management regulation

Despite the aforementioned differences in the type of regulation, the general objective of the regulatory approaches is similar. The legislative or privately set rules are primarily serving to protect investors. This goal has a high priority especially in the Anglo-Saxon countries. As the protection of investors is aided by reliable financial reporting, an internal control system ensuring the reliability of financial reporting is of particular relevance. In Germany, however, § 91 par. 2 AktG has a broader scope; it requires a general risk management system to identify developments that might threaten the going concern of the firm. Thus, the regulation also aims to protect creditors. In Japan, the risk management system is supposed to ensure that firms are better able to fulfil their obligations to the society.

Due to these differences, the type of firms impacted by the risk management regulation varies. In the USA, UK and Australia, the regulatory requirements target only listed companies. § 91 par. 2 AktG, on the contrary, concerns all German stock corporations and, in addition, applies to certain firms with other legal forms (e.g. large public limited companies). The Japanese rules for risk management are not confined to listed stock corporations either, but rather concern all stock corporations. The corporate governance codes of Germany and Japan, however, focus primarily on listed firms. As regards other (non-binding) standards on risk management, the scope is not limited to a particular group of firms.

The legal rules, corporate governance codes and other pronouncements on risk management have generally to be applied group-wide. It is not clear-cut, though, whether joint ventures and associates have to be integrated into the group-wide risk management system in addition to subsidiaries. While the British Turnbull Report and the Australian Corporate Governance Principles explicitly require their integration if they are material, an interpretation of the law is necessary in Germany. This interpretation leads to the conclusion that at least material joint ventures should be integrated into the group-wide risk management system.

Another key aspect is the definition of the required systems as regards form and content. Such a definition is complicated by terminological differences and the use of undefined legal terms. In general, two views can be distinguished: on the one hand, the risk management system (RMS) is subsumed under the internal control system (ICS). This view was shaped by the broad definition of internal control in the first COSO Report (COSO, 1992). It has been adopted in the auditing standard for the internal control system of the Chartered Institute of Auditors in Germany (IDW PS 260) as well as in the Turnbull Report in the United Kingdom. On the other hand, there is an opposing view that the risk management system comprises the internal control system. This definition can be found in the Australian Corporate Governance Code and the second COSO Report, 'Enterprise Risk Management – Integrated Framework' (COSO, 2004). Although such differences are of a formal nature, they impair the development of a common understanding of risk management.

The problem of defining the content can be illustrated by the example of § 302 SOX and § 91 par. 2 AktG. German companies that are listed in the United States, and are thus under the supervision of the SEC, have to comply with both regulations. Consequently, the relationship between these rules becomes of interest. In particular, the question arises whether or not the requirements of § 302 SOX are broader in scope than those of § 91 par. 2 AktG. In the literature, different views are held in this respect. On the one hand, it is argued that the SOX is broader as it refers to all material information while the German law is confined to information on developments that might endanger the going concern (e.g. Lanfermann and Maul, 2002). On the other hand, it is argued that the German regulation is more comprehensive because it does not focus only on the information necessary for financial reporting and is not limited to consolidated companies (e.g. Ballwieser and Dobler, 2003). As the legal norms are not clearly defined in both cases, the definition of the systems and their relationship is subject to interpretation.

The comparison further reveals that the term 'risk' is neither defined in the laws nor in the corporate governance codes. In the professional standards, however, risk is defined in different ways (Table 1.2). While the COSO (enterprise risk management) Framework is based on the understanding of risk as downside risk, the Australian and Japanese standards follow a broad definition that includes both upside and downside risk, that is positive and negative deviations from a target.

Differences in the national regulations can also be observed as regards external reporting on risk management. In Germany, for instance, a description of the risk management system is mandatory in the statutory group management report according to German Accounting Standard No. 5 (GAS 5), while such a description is only recommended in Japan. The American regulation requires a report on the internal control over financial reporting which has to be audited by the external auditor. A description of the general risk management system, however, is not compulsory.

Finally, some country-specific particularities can be observed. In Germany, for example, the risk management systems of listed companies are subject to a mandatory audit by external auditors (§ 317 par. 4 HGB – German Commercial Code). Specifying this legal requirement, the auditing standard IDW PS 340 defines three audit criteria: the existence of the system, the effectiveness of the system's design, and the system's operating effectiveness (Dobler, 2004, p. 53ff.). In the United States and Australia, the CEO and CFO of listed firms have to confirm that they have established internal control systems. Such a confirmation will become compulsory in the EU (European Union) as well, because the amended accounting directives now require a statement on corporate governance, a requirement that member states have to transform into national law by 2008.

After this broad overview of risk management regulation in major industrial countries the following section presents risk management as an element of corporate governance in more detail. For this purpose, the regulatory risk management requirements in Germany and the United Kingdom are outlined and

Table 1.2 Objectives and contents of the risk management regulation

	Germany	UK	USA	Australia	Japan
Key regulation	§ 91 par. 2 AktG	The Combined Code on Corporate Governance	§§ 302 and 404 SOA	ASX Principles of Good Corporate Governance	§§ 21–7 Special Exceptions Law for the Commercial Code
Primary goal	Protect shareholders and creditors	Protect investors	Protect investors	Protect investors	Protect investors; fulfil obligations to society
Companies concerned	Stock corporations; selective application on companies with other legal form	Listed stock corporations	Listed stock corporations	Listed stock corporations	Stock corporations
Group-wide scope	Subsidiaries that might threaten the parent's going concern; main joint ventures and in certain cases associates	Subsidiaries, main joint ventures and associates	Consolidated subsidiaries	Subsidiaries, main joint ventures and associates	Subsidiaries
Relationship between RMS and ICS	RMS is part of ICS	RMS is part of ICS	COSO Internal Control: RMS is part of ICS COSO ERM Framework: ICS is part of ERM	ICS is part of RMS	ICS and RMS complement each other

(continued)

Table 1.2 (*Continued*)

	Germany	UK	USA	Australia	Japan
Definition of risk	§ 91 par. 2 AktG: no definition of risk; the term 'developments that might threaten the firm's existence' is subject to interpretation	Combined Code and Turnbull Report: no definition of risk	SOX: no definition of risk COSO Internal Control: no definition of risk COSO ERM Framework: 'risk is the possibility that an event will occur and adversely affect the achievement of objectives'	ASX Principles of Good Corporate Governance: no definition of risk AS/NZS 4360:2004: 'The chance of something happening that will have an impact upon objectives.'	§§ 21–7 Special Exceptions Law for the Commercial Code: no definition of risk JIS Q 2001: 'A combination of the probability of an event and its consequence' METI Study Group: 'uncertainty of occurrence of an event'
Risk type	Downside risk	Downside risk	Downside risk	Up- and downside risk	Up- and downside risk
External Reporting on risk management	Description of the risk management system in the group management report (GAS 5)	Statement on Internal Control: Confirmation that a risk management process is established	Internal Control Report: Evaluation of the effectiveness of the internal control over financial reporting	Description of the risk management policy and of the internal control system	Report on risk management and internal control recommended
Particularities	Mandatory external audit of the risk management system of listed firms (§ 317 par. 4 HGB; IDW PS 340)	–	Statement on internal control over financial reporting by the CEO and CFO Audit of the Internal Control Report by the external auditor (PCAOB Auditing Standard No. 2)	Statement on the risk management and internal control system by the CEO and CFO	–

discussed. These two countries are of particular interest because of their different corporate governance systems.

Risk management as an element of corporate governance and internal control

Risk management in the German two-tier board system

The legal requirement to establish a risk management system according to § 91 par. 2 AktG is accompanied by several other legal and professional norms. It is the common objective of these regulations to ensure a proper governance of the firm. The norms have been defined in view of the German two-tier board system (Figure 1.1). In this system of corporate governance, the management and supervision of the company are separated in two independent boards (Cromme, 2005). The management board of a German stock corporation is responsible for managing the firm. The supervisory board, on the contrary, monitors the management board. It appoints the members of the management board, assigns the auditor and reports to the general assembly of shareholders.

§ 91 par. 2 AktG requires that the management board 'takes appropriate measures, in particular to establish a monitoring system, to early identify developments that might endanger the going concern of the firm'. This rather vague

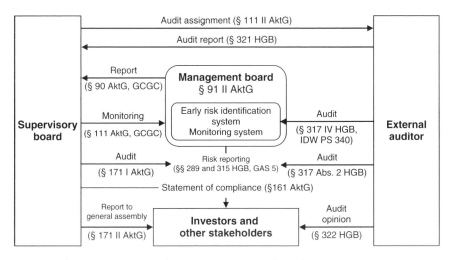

Figure 1.1 Risk management in the German two-tier board system

wording of the law has been subject to interpretation (Weber and Liekweg, 2005). In general, a two-step obligation is derived from this regulation:

- First, the management board must take appropriate measures to early identify risks that threaten the existence of the firm (early risk identification system).
- Second, the management board must monitor the effectiveness of these measures (internal monitoring system).

Both systems are referred to as a 'risk management system'. It is important to note, however, that the response to identified risks (risk control system) is not part of the requirements according to § 91 par. 2 AktG. Taking risks and responding to them is rather within the discretion of the management board. It would constitute an offence against the duty of due care, though, to take risks that are either inappropriate or are endangering the going concern.

§ 91 par. 2 AktG emphasises a specific aspect of the general duty to lead the firm (§ 76 AktG) and specifies the duty of due care (§ 93 par. 1 AktG). The German Corporate Governance Code underlines this task: 'The Management Board ensures appropriate risk management and risk controlling in the enterprise.' (par. 4.1.4). As risk management is part of the general tasks of the management board, the supervisory board has to monitor the risk management of the firm. This requires regular information about the risk exposure and the risk management processes. For this reason, the German Corporate Governance Code requires that the 'Management Board informs the Supervisory Board regularly, without delay and comprehensively, of all issues important to the enterprise with regard to . . . risk situation and risk management' (par. 3.4). The statutory report of the management board to the supervisory board forms a basis for this (§ 90 AktG).

In the case of a listed firm, the early risk identification and internal monitoring system are subject to a mandatory external audit (§ 317 par. 4 HGB). The results of the audit are reported in a separate part of the audit report (§ 321 par. 4 HGB). In this internal report, which is addressed to the supervisory board, the external auditor must mention any improvements that are necessary in relation to the risk management system. Specific suggestions are not required in the audit report, though they can be included in the management letter. The audit opinion does not entail any information about the audit of the risk management system because it only confirms compliance with financial accounting rules (§ 322 HGB). The establishment of a risk management system, however, is an organisational duty of the management board. This may be criticised as investors and other stakeholders are consequently not informed about the results of the external audit of the risk management system.

The external audit and its results constitute an important basis for the monitoring tasks of the supervisory board. It receives, in addition to the regular reports by the management board, an independent opinion about the effectiveness of the risk management system. The supervisory board can thus direct its monitoring activities on specific issues and can agree a specific audit focus with the external auditor as part of the audit assignment. The mandatory audit by the external auditor is no substitute for the supervisory board's own monitoring activities. These include, in addition to the audit scope of the external auditor, the efficiency of the early risk identification and internal monitoring system as well as the measures taken by the management board in response to identified risks. Moreover, the supervisory board can declare that particular risky transactions need its prior approval (§ 111 par. 4 AktG).

The German Corporate Governance Code further specifies the tasks of the supervisory board: the chairman of the supervisory board shall consult the management board regarding risk management (par. 5.2) and the supervisory board shall set up an audit committee (par. 5.3.2) that handles – among other issues – issues of risk management. These provisions of the German Corporate Governance Code are supported by the joint statement of compliance that the management board and the supervisory board of listed companies have to publish annually (§ 161 AktG).

In addition to establishing a risk management system the management board has to report on the material risks and opportunities in the statutory management report (§§ 289, 315 HGB). This requirement is specified by the German Accounting Standard No. 5 (GAS 5) 'Risk Reporting' (Kajüter, 2006). According to this standard, all material risks that might affect the decisions of the users of the management report shall be disclosed and possible consequences described. Risks threatening the going concern of the enterprise must be clearly described as such (GAS 5.15). Moreover, GAS 5.28 requires that the risk management system is described adequately. An example for such a description is presented in Box 1.1. As the management report is subject to an external audit, the auditor must check if the risks and opportunities are fairly presented. The auditor must explicitly address risks that might threaten the going concern in its audit opinion and has to confirm that the risks and opportunities are fairly presented (§ 322 par. 2 and 3 HGB).

Box 1.1 Report on the risk management system by HOCHTIEF AG (Annual Report 2006, p. 85f)

Unified early warning system throughout the HOCHTIEF Group

A Group-wide directive lays down standard procedures for risk management. The divisions supplement this directive with organizational instructions geared to their specific circumstances.

Risks are inventoried at all operating locations and aggregated to Group level. This approach makes it possible to involve managers at all levels of the corporate hierarchy, ensuring that risk awareness is all-pervasive from project managers all the way through to divisional heads and holding company executives.

All risks are assigned an impact, probability, category, timescale and action to be taken. In complement to this quantitatively focused reporting, HOCHTIEF also attaches great importance to open discussion of risks by management. A key element of our early warning system is therefore a dedicated Risk Management Steering Committee made up of divisional and corporate center representatives. This panel looks at reported risks from the differing perspectives of the divisions and the holding company, allowing all material risks to be evaluated in an integrated framework. The Steering Committee also coordinates and adopts binding countermeasures.

HOCHTIEF compiles the Steering Committee's findings in a risk situation analysis. This details all major risks in tabular form. The commented analysis forms an integral part of reporting by the Controlling function and is finalized by the Executive Board. The Controlling function also reports on opportunities. There is no offsetting of risks and opportunities.

. . .

Risk management audit

The auditors examined the early warning system and its integration into planning and reporting processes when auditing the annual financial statements. Their review shows that the Executive Board has taken appropriate measures to set up a system for the early detection of risk as stipulated by Sec. 91 (2) of the German Stock Corporations Act (AktG). In addition, this early warning system is fundamentally capable of identifying at an early stage any development that might cast doubt over the Group's ability to continue as a going concern.

Our internal auditing function additionally reviews and evaluates the proper functioning and cost-effectiveness of the installed systems and processes. Identified scope for improvement is presented in the Risk Management Steering Committee and incorporated in refinements to the risk management system.

Due to the abstract wording of § 91 par. 2 AktG, the legal requirement was subject to interpretation. There has been a controversial discussion between academia (both management and law scientists) and the auditing profession in particular about the type of risks that have to be identified, assessed and reported to the management board. On the one hand, management academics and the auditing profession hold the view that § 91 par. 2 AktG requires the identification, assessment and reporting of all material individual risks. According to this view, it is not sufficient to focus on risks that endanger the going concern because individual risks might have cumulative effects and might interrelate with other individual risks so that the going concern is threatened. On the other hand, this wide interpretation of the law is criticised by law academics. They argue that the law only refers to 'developments' and that it would therefore be sufficient that the management board is able to assess the risk situation in general. As it is practically almost impossible to focus a risk management system only on risks that endanger the going concern, companies have followed the opinion of their external auditors and have established risk management systems that record individual risks.

The internal monitoring system which ensures the effectiveness of the early risk identification system is less controversial, although the law does not define specific requirements in this respect. It is therefore for the management board to decide which measures are most appropriate. In general, there are two measures that are not exclusive: integrated controls (e.g. for meeting deadlines of risk reports) and internal audits. The latter can be carried out by an internal audit function. Although the establishment of an internal audit function is not required by law, it is recommended by professional bodies such as the Schmalenbach-Gesellschaft in Germany. The role of internal auditors has gained relevance as a result of § 91 par. 2 AktG and in their audit they can refer to a specific auditing standard issued by The German Institute of Internal Auditors.

Risk management in the UK one-tier board system

In the United Kingdom, there is no legal obligation for firms to establish a risk management system. However, for listed companies the Combined Code on Corporate Governance requires a system of internal control which comprises a risk management system. Guidance on this matter is provided by the Turnbull Report on Internal Control (Financial Reporting Council, 2005a; Blackburn, 1999). Both pronouncements refer to the UK one-tier board system. This system of corporate governance assigns the responsibility for leading the firm and monitoring the management to the Board of Directors. Within the board, there are two types of directors: executive and non-executive directors. To work effectively, the board establishes committees for specific tasks (e.g. the audit committee, nomination committee, remuneration committee, etc.).

The Financial Reporting Council has, as one of its roles as an independent regulator, to maintain the Combined Code on Corporate Governance. The latest version of the Combined Code was published in 2006 following relatively minor amendments to the 2003 version. The Combined Code operates on what is referred to as a 'comply or explain' basis. That is, under UK Listing Rules a UK-listed company must either state in the annual report that they have complied with the Combined Code, or they must explain which provisions they have not complied with and why they have chosen not to comply with them. Non-UK companies listed in the UK must explain how their corporate governance approach varies from the Combined Code and state if their approach complies with the corporate governance regime within its own country. This principles-based approach allows companies to depart from the Combined Code should they feel it is appropriate, whilst also requiring those companies to explain why their individual circumstances require an alternative governance approach. Within the Code the board's responsibilities in respect of internal control are set out in Section C.2 (Box 1.2).

Box 1.2 Internal control provisions in The Combined Code on Corporate Governance (Financial Reporting Council 2006, p. 14)

Main Principle

C.2 The Board should maintain a sound system of internal control to safeguard shareholders' investment and the company's assets.

Code Provision

C.2.1 The board should, at least annually, conduct a review of the effectiveness of the group's internal controls and should report to shareholders that they have done so. The review should cover all material controls, including financial, operational and compliance controls and risk management systems.

In addition the Combined Code establishes that one of the responsibilities of the audit committee is 'to review the company's internal financial controls and... to review the company's internal control and risk management systems' (Financial Reporting Council, 2006, p. 15). These provisions relating to internal control and risk management are, prima facie, relatively straightforward and undemanding. There is, however, further best practice provided on how to apply the Code under the Turnbull Guidance on Internal Control (Financial Reporting Council, 2005a) and the Smith Guidance on Audit Committees (Financial Reporting Council, 2005b), both of which continue to adopt a principles-based approach.

The Turnbull guidance establishes that a system of internal control embraces not solely the control procedures, but also the policies and behaviours that are necessary to ensure such a system can successfully protect assets and manage risks. The responsibility for embedding such a system within the culture of the company lies primarily with the board of directors, but there is acknowledgement that all employees have some part to play in the operation of an internal control system. It is emphasised that the annual review of the effectiveness of the internal control system is central to the board's responsibilities and therefore a process must be established to assess the quality of the following: the risk management system and associated controls, the work of the internal audit function, and the ability of the company to respond to risks. Whereas the Combined Code only requires the company to disclose within the annual report that the board has completed a review of the effectiveness of the internal control system, the Turnbull guidance recommends additional disclosures on internal control. The further disclosures expected within a statement on internal control are: an outline of the principal features of the risk management and internal control system, an explanation that a process exists to identify and manage the company's main risks, a statement that the board has responsibility for the effectiveness review and a summary of the review process, confirmation that actions have been undertaken in respect of any weaknesses in the system and an explanation that the system cannot eliminate risk rather it can only manage risk. There is, however, no requirement to comment upon the effectiveness of the internal control system. Box 1.3 shows the internal control statement of TESCO plc. as an example.

Box 1.3 Statement on Internal Control of TESCO plc (Annual Report 2006, p. 22f)

Risk management and internal control

... the Board has overall responsibility for risk management and internal control within the context of achieving the Group's objectives. Executive management is responsible for defining and maintaining the necessary control systems. The role of internal audit is to monitor the overall system and report on its effectiveness. ...

The Board maintains a Key Risk Register which we review formally twice a year. The register is populated with risks identified through discussions principally between the Head of Internal Audit and the Board of Directors although the views of senior management are also invited. Collectively, the Board conduct an assessment of risk severity, considering impact and likelihood and the adequacy of mitigating measures taken by the business. ...

This process is cascaded through the Group with every International CEO and local Board conducting and maintaining their own risk register and assessing their own control systems. The same process also applies functionally in those parts of the Group requiring greater overview. For example, its terms of reference require the Audit Committee to oversee the Finance Risk Register. A further example is that of the Corporate

Responsibility Register which specifically considers social, ethical and environmental (SEE) risks. . . .

Accountability for managing risk at an operational level sits with management. We have a Group-wide process for establishing clearly the risks and responsibilities assigned to each level of management and the expected controls required to be operated and monitored.

The CEOs of subsidiary businesses are required to certify by way of annual statements of assurance that the Board's governance policies have been adopted in practice and in spirit. For certain joint ventures, the Board places reliance upon the systems of internal control operating within our partners' infrastructure and the obligations upon partners' Boards relating to the effectiveness of their own systems. . . .

Annually, the Audit Committee reports to the Board on its review of the effectiveness of the internal control systems for the accounting year and the period to the date of approval of the financial statements. . . .

It should be understood that such systems are designed to provide reasonable, but not absolute, assurance against material mis-statement or loss.

The Smith guidance places responsibility for reviewing the risk management and internal control system onto the audit committee unless a separate board risk management committee has been established and charged with this role. The audit committee does not have to adopt responsibility for reviewing the effectiveness of the risk management and internal control system except where this is expressly stated to be a part of its role; if the audit committee does not have this responsibility then it is considered to be a management role. In the latter situation the audit committee should be receiving relevant reports from management, internal auditors and the external auditors concerning the effectiveness of the internal control systems. The audit committee is also tasked with reviewing the annual report disclosure statements on internal control. In group situations the parent company audit committee reviews internal control and risk management issues in subsidiary companies. The Smith guidance does stress that 'Nothing in the guidance should be interpreted as a departure from the principle of the unitary board. All directors remain equally responsible for the company's affairs as a matter of law. The audit committee remains a committee of the board' (Financial Reporting Council, 2005b, p. 3).

The role of the external auditor in relation to the internal control and risk management system is set out in the Listing Rules. The Listing Rules require the external auditor to review whether the company has complied with the internal control provisions C.2.1 of the Code before the annual report has been published. The Auditing Practices Board (APB) has issued Bulletin 2006/2005 that provides guidance to external auditors concerning the review. The auditor's objective is to 'assess whether the company's summary of the process the board. . . has adopted in reviewing the effectiveness of the system of internal control, is both supported by the documentation prepared by or for the directors and appropriately reflects that process' (APB Bulletin 2006/5, p. 11). Importantly there is no requirement for the external auditors to form an opinion upon the effectiveness of the company's internal controls, although any weaknesses in internal controls that are identified during the audit should be reported to the directors. Consequently the approach to risk management in the UK can be summarised in Figure 1.2.

Organisations such as the Institute of Internal Auditors have sometimes criticised the Turnbull guidance on the grounds that its highly generalised nature means there are issues surrounding the definition of key terms and phrases. For example, there is a lack of clarity as to how 'effectiveness' should be interpreted or how the process of reviewing effectiveness should be performed (Institute of Internal Auditors, 2005). However, the generic nature of the guidance is also seen as a strength in that it enables all types of company to apply its provisions.

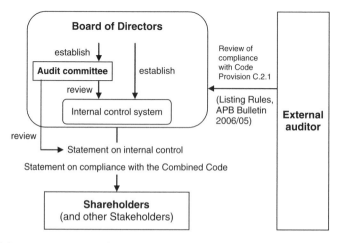

Figure 1.2 Risk management in the British one-tier board system

In collecting evidence for the 2005 review of the Turnbull guidance it was generally acknowledged that the Turnbull guidance has assisted in improving risk management practices in the United Kingdom with a majority of UK listed companies reporting that risk management and internal control systems are now integrated into their standard business practices (Financial Reporting Council, 2005c). The positive responses received in gathering evidence for the review included comments such as 'we believe that the Turnbull guidance has been one of the most successful additions to the UK corporate governance framework and has succeeded in meeting its stated objectives of remaining relevant over time' (Financial Reporting Council, 2005c, p. 6) and the evidence does appear to vindicate the adoption of a principles-based approach.

Comparison of the German and UK risk management regulation

The requirements in respect of risk management and internal control systems in Germany and the UK certainly differ, and at first sight these differences appear to be significant. For example, there is a legal requirement to establish a risk management system in Germany, but there is no such requirement in the UK. The external auditors must audit the early risk identification and internal monitoring system of listed firms in Germany, but in the UK the auditor checks for compliance with the internal control provisions of the Combined Code on Corporate Governance. There is a risk-related accounting standard in Germany, but no such equivalent in the UK. These differences may not be as large as they initially appear however, and thus even though there is a two-tier board system operation in Germany and a one-tier system in the UK its impact upon risk management and internal control regimes may not be as large as expected.

The governance regimes that operate in the two countries share an overall objective which is to ensure that companies are managed effectively. An important aspect of the sound management of a company is that an appropriate system of internal control and risk management exists. Consequently, although there is no legal requirement to implement a risk management system in the UK it is a main principle of the corporate governance code that such a system exists. In practical terms therefore, although the type of risk management is not prescribed, it is inconceivable that a listed UK company could operate without a risk management system.

The separation of the management board and the supervisory board in Germany does entail that their respective responsibilities are carefully demarcated through legislation and through the German Corporate Governance Code. Thus the management board establishes the system for the early identification of risks and monitors the effectiveness of the system; whereas the supervisory board monitors how well this role is being performed by the management board. In the UK, the board of directors are responsible for those tasks undertaken by the management board in Germany, whereas in the UK the audit committee is responsible for those tasks undertaken by the supervisory board in Germany. It is the case that in the UK members of the audit committee are drawn from the board of directors, unlike Germany where the members of the supervisory board are independent from the management board. This autonomy may be considered beneficial in making the management board more accountable, but the division of responsibilities that occurs is similar.

The difference in the respective roles of the external auditors in the two countries is perhaps not as wide as it first appears either. For the UK auditor to state whether there has been compliance with the provisions of the Combined Code requires a review of relevant supporting documentation and an assessment of whether it supports the board's statement that they have conducted a review of the effectiveness of the system of internal controls. Thus whilst it is not a mandatory audit of the risk system as in Germany that is occurring, the UK auditor's review of compliance is more extensive than initially may be thought.

On the other hand, the different corporate governance systems have an impact on the internal audit function. In Germany, internal auditors report to the management board. If they are charged with auditing the risk management system, they therefore inform the management board about the results of their audit. In the UK, internal auditors usually report to the audit committee. As a consequence, the audit committee has direct access to the internal audit function and can refer to the results of the internal audit which facilitates its monitoring task. Such a direct reporting of internal auditors to the supervisory board or its audit committee would be inconsistent with the German two-tier board system, however. It might impair the relationship of trust between the management board and the internal audit function. There has been a controversial debate about this matter in Germany, however, because the results of the internal audit may be useful for the supervisory board in monitoring the risk management system. For this reason, it is in general considered to be consistent with the two-tier board system if a representative of the internal audit function participates in the meetings of the supervisory board. In recent years, it has also become more common in German firms that the internal audit function informs the audit committee. Thus, as the corporate governance systems are converging, differences in risk management regimes are declining.

Finally, the scope of companies affected by the regulation differs. While the requirement to establish a risk management system according to § 91 par. 2 AktG applies to all stock corporations and certain firms with other legal forms, the provisions of the Combined Code have been designed for listed companies. This might imply that a German parent company that buys a British non-listed firm might not find a well-developed risk management system as it might expect from the German perspective. On the other hand, if a British non-listed parent company buys a German stock corporation, it might be surprised to find a formal risk management system even though the stock corporation is not listed.

Conclusions

National governments, standard setters and professional bodies around the world have responded to an increasing number of corporate failures and bankruptcies by specifying the rules for risk management. The regulations define minimum standards for dealing with risk. Influenced by different legal traditions, the type of regulation varies internationally (legislation *vs.* soft law). As a result, there are – at least formally – differences in the degree of binding of risk management regulation across countries. Moreover, the type of companies affected by the regulation and the scope of the required systems varies as well.

As risk management regulations often apply to listed companies, firms may be affected by foreign national regulatory requirements when they file for a listing at a stock exchange in another country. The SOX is an example in this respect.

Many of the regulations analysed above are relatively new. Their impact on corporate governance and risk management practice needs further in-depth research in the future (Fédération des Experts Comptables Européens, 2005). In particular international comparisons of risk management regulations and risk management practice might provide valuable insights and deepen our understanding in this area.

References

Association of Insurance and Risk Managers (2002). *A Risk Management Standard.* Association of Insurance and Risk Managers/Association of Local Authority Risk Managers/Institute of Risk Managers, London.

APB Bulletin (2006/2005). The Combined Code on Corporate Governance: Requirements of Auditors under the Listing Rules of the Financial Services authority and the Irish Stock Exchange, FRC publications.

ASX Corporate Governance Council (2003). Principles of Good Corporate Governance and Best Practice Recommendations, Sydney.

Ballwieser, W. and Dobler, M. (2003). 'Bilanzdelikte: Konsequenzen, Ursachen und Maßnahmen zu ihrer Vermeidung', *Die Unternehmung*, Vol. 57, No. 6, pp. 449–469.

Blackburn, S. (1999). Managing Risk and Achieving Turnbull Compliance, in: Accountant's Digest, No. 417, London.

Chenhall, R.H. (2003). 'Management control systems design within its organizational context: findings from contingency-based research and directions for the future', *Accounting, Organizations and Society*, Vol. 28, pp. 127–168.

Committee of Sponsoring Organisations of the Treadway Commission (COSO) (1992). *Internal Control – Integrated Framework*, AICPA, New York, NY.

Committee of Sponsoring Organisations of the Treadway Commission (COSO) (2004). *Enterprise Risk Management – Integrated Framework*. AICPA, New York, NY.

Cromme, G. (2005). 'Corporate Governance in Germany and the German Corporate Governance Code', *Corporate Governance: An International Journal*, Vol. 13, No. 3, pp. 362–367.

Dobler, M. (2004). 'Auditing Corporate Risk Management – A Critical Analysis of a German Particularity', *The ICFAI Journal of Audit Practice*, Vol. 1, pp. 49–64.

Doherty, N.A. (2000). *Integrated Risk Management*. McGraw Hill, New York.

Fama, E.F. (1980). 'Agency Problems and the Theory of the Firm', *Journal of Political Economy*, Vol. 88, S. 288–307.

Fédération des Experts Comptables Européens (2005): Risk Management and Internal Control in the EU. Discussion Paper, available online: www.fee.be (17.05.2007).

Financial Reporting Council (2005a). Internal Control: Revised Guidance for Directors on the Combined Code, London.

Financial Reporting Council (2005b). Guidance on Audit Committees (The Smith Guidance), London.

Financial Reporting Council (2005c). Review of Turnbull Guidance on Internal Control – Evidence Paper, London.

Financial Reporting Council (2006). The Combined Code on Corporate Governance, London.

Government Commission German Corporate Governance Code (2006): German Corporate Governance Code (version 2006), available online: www.corporate-governance-code.de (17.05.2007).

Group of 100 (2003). Guide to Compliance with ASX Principle 7: 'Recognise and Manage Risks', Melbourne.

Institute of Internal Auditors (2005). Response to the Review of the Turnbull Guidance on Internal Control.

Japanese Standards Association (2001). *JIS Q 2001: Guidelines for Development and Implementation of Risk Management System*, Tokyo.

Jensen, M.C. and Meckling, W.H. (1976). 'Theory of the firm: Managerial behavior, agency costs and ownership structure', *Journal of Financial Economics*, Vol. 3, pp. 305–360.

Kajüter, P. (2006). Risk disclosures of listed firms in Germany: A longitudinal study. Paper presented at the Tenth Financial Reporting & Business Communication Conference, Cardiff.

Lanfermann, G. and Maul, S. (2002). 'Auswirkungen des Sarbanes-Oxley Acts in Deutschland', *Der Betrieb*, Vol. 55, No. 34, pp. 1725–1732.

METI Study Group (2003): Internal Control in the New Era of Risks – Guidelines for Internal Control That Functions Together with Risk Management.

Otley, D.T. (1980). 'The contingency theory of management accounting: achievement and prognosis', *Accounting, Organizations and Society*, Vol. 4, p. 413–428.

Ross, S.A. (1973). The Economic Theory of Agency: The Principle's Problem, in: Fels, R. and Thweatt, W.O. (eds), The American Economic Review: Papers and Proceedings of the Eighty-fifth Annual Meeting of the American Economic Association, Toronto, pp. 134–139.

Stulz, R.M. (1996). 'Rethinking Risk Management', *Journal of Applied Corporate Finance*, Vol. 9, No. 3, 1996, pp. 8–24.

Tokyo Stock Exchange (2004). Principles of Corporate Governance for Listed Companies, Tokyo.

Tufano, P. (1998). 'Agency Costs of Corporate Risk Management', *Financial Management*, Vol. 27, No. 1, pp. 67–77.

Ugochukwu Uche, C. (2001). 'The theory of regulation: A review article', in: *Journal of Financial Regulation and Compliance*, Vol. 9, No. 1, pp. 67–80.

Waterhouse, J. and Tiessen, P. (1978). 'A contingency framework for management accounting systems research', *Accounting, Organizations and Society*, Vol. 3, pp. 65–76.

Weber, J. and Liekweg, A. (2005). Statutory Regulation of the Risk Management Function in Germany: Implementation Issues for the Non-Financial Sector, in Frenkel, M., Hommel, U. and Rudolf, M. (eds), *Risk Management*, 2. ed., Springer, Berlin, pp. 495–511.

A Commentary on the COSO Internal Control Framework and its links with Sarbanes–Oxley

Margaret Woods

Nottingham University Business School, UK

Introduction

Both definitions of risk and our understanding of the term risk management have evolved over time, such that Selim and McNamee (1999, p. 161) note what they describe as 'major paradigm shifts in organizations' approach to risk management.' In pre-rationalism times risk was seen as a consequence of natural causes that could not be anticipated or managed, but more modern, scientific-based thinking has led to the emergence of a view that risk is both quantifiable and manageable via the judicious use of avoidance and protection strategies.

More recently, risk management has evolved from an insurance and transaction-based function into a broader concept that is linked to both corporate governance and strategic planning (Unsworth, 1995; McLave, 1996; Nottingham, 1997). This shift is in part due to a broadening of the definition of risk, which now extends beyond the boundaries of financial risk to encompass issues such as corporate reputation, regulatory compliance, health and safety of employees, supply chain management and general operational activities. Risk is now viewed from a very broad perspective, and this changed perspective has led to some rethinking of the approaches to the design of internal control systems.

In the United States, the Committee of Sponsoring Organizations (COSO) has published two key reports (COSO, 1992 and 2004) laying down guidelines on the design of internal control systems. The aim of this chapter is to offer a commentary on the evolution of the COSO guidelines and discuss the way in which they have been used to help frame regulations in the USA. The chapter also discusses the way in which the COSO 1992 Framework was integrated into implementation guidelines for Section 404 of the Sarbanes–Oxley Act (SOX) 2002, and the problems that have arisen out of Section 404. This leads into debate over the question of the different interpretations of internal control implied by Section 404 as opposed to Enterprise Risk Management (ERM). The chapter ends with a brief review of the current position within the European Union (EU) in terms of the desirability of opting for SOX-style regulations, or taking a softer approach to encouraging management to ensure their companies utilize effective internal control systems. I conclude that approaches to guidance and regulation on risk and control are globally diverse, and the prospects for convergence are uncertain. The only firm point of agreement is that risk management and effective internal control are fundamental prerequisites of good corporate governance.

Historical background

The origins of the COSO Framework for enterprise risk management, and the complementary pressures to ensure reliable financial reporting under the SOX (2002), henceforth referred to as SOX, lie in the Foreign Corrupt Practices Act (FCPA) of 1977. This act was intended to correct the financial reporting ills of that time, and it included broad-based provisions designed to enhance internal control systems within public companies (Shank and Miguel, 2006).

The Committee of Sponsoring Organizations (COSO) was established 8 years later in 1985 as a voluntary private sector initiative to sponsor the National Commission on Fraudulent Financial Reporting. The aim was to identify the causes of fraudulent financial reporting and develop recommendations for public companies and their independent auditors, as well as for the SEC, other regulators and also educational institutions.

The organizations that sponsored the National Commission were the American Accounting Association, the American Institute of Certified Public Accountants, Financial Executives International, The Institute of Internal Auditors, and the National Association of Accountants (now the Institute of Management Accountants). The Chairman of the Commission was James C. Treadway, Jr, a former Commissioner of the US Securities and Exchange Commission, and the other commission members comprised representatives from industry, the New York Stock Exchange and professional accounting and investment firms.

The Report of the National Commission on Fraudulent Financial Reporting, often referred to as the Treadway commission, was published in 1987. The report recommended that the sponsoring organizations work together to develop guidelines on internal control for public companies, and this led to the publication of the 1992 report entitled 'Internal Control – Integrated Framework' (COSO, 1992). This report presented a common definition of internal control and provided a framework for the assessment and improvement of internal control systems.

COSO 1992

The COSO report views internal control as a process designed to provide reasonable assurance regarding the achievement of three core objectives:

1. Effectiveness and efficiency of operations
2. Reliability of financial reporting
3. Compliance with laws and regulations.

By implication, internal control is classed as being effective if the Board of Directors has reasonable assurance that the above three objectives are being achieved.

Whilst the COSO report acknowledges that the term internal control may mean different things to different people, it also defines internal control as being characterized as comprising five inter-related components. The five elements are as follows:

1. Control environment
2. Risk assessment
3. Control activities
4. Information and communication
5. Monitoring.

It is useful to look at each of these components in a little more detail.

Control environment

Responsibility for the creation of the control environment rests with the Board of Directors and the environment is described by COSO as setting the tone of the organization and the control awareness of its staff. In so doing, it serves as the foundation for all other components of internal control. In other words, if the management philosophy is one which is supportive of personal integrity and well-defined control systems, then this culture will permeate the whole of the internal control system. The Board of Directors are responsible for creating the necessary structures, policy formulation and appointment of the necessary staff to ensure that business controls are in place to ensure achievement of the core objectives of effective operations, reliable financial reporting and compliance.

Risk assessment

Organizations face a broad range of both external and internally generated risks that may impede the achievement of their objectives. Risk assessment involves the identification and evaluation of these risks, so that a framework can be constructed to ensure that they are managed effectively. Good control requires an understanding of which risks are most significant in terms of the threat they pose to organizational objectives, as well as the mechanisms to review how the pattern of risks may change over time.

Control activities

An integral part of internal control is the design of mechanisms that check the effective operation of business processes, to minimize the risk of both error and fraud. The controls are spread across all levels of an organization; they may be formal or informal, financial or non-financial and quantitative or qualitative in nature, but are all designed with a common aim. The aim is to provide an assurance that business processes are operating in a way that will ensure achievement of organizational objectives. The range of controls may include spending approvals, reconciliations, segregation of duties, access controls and so on.

Information and communication

The likelihood of achieving organizational objectives is dependent, in part, upon decision-making which is based upon accurate information. It is therefore vital that the internal controls are designed in such a way that managers have access to timely and accurate reports on the operational, financial and compliance issues, which can facilitate an evaluation of the extent to which performance is on target. Such performance reports will encompass both internal and external issues, and they serve to ensure that the control system rapidly pinpoints errors or irregularities, and that the findings are communicated to a manager or other member of staff who can take corrective action. The COSO report emphasizes the point that good communication is indicative that staff take their control responsibilities seriously, and that communication should not just be in an upward direction but also with external parties such as customers, suppliers, regulators and shareholders.

Monitoring

Efforts devoted to the introduction of an internal control system may prove to be worthless if the controls are ineffective. COSO therefore identifies monitoring of the control system as the final component of internal control. Such monitoring may be continuous or discrete but the extent of monitoring should reflect the level of associated risk. It is this type of thinking that forms the basis of the risk-based approaches to internal audit that are now in widespread use. Control failures or deficiencies need to be rectified and it is therefore important that the monitoring process is complemented by a system for reporting such problems upwards to senior management.

The five components of internal control should not be viewed as discrete elements, but as connected mechanisms that work in combination to provide assurance about the three core objectives. Each objective requires that all five components are present, and this is most effectively achieved when the controls are built into the organizational infrastructure such that control is not a separate consideration, but is instead a part of the 'essence' of the business.

In addition to highlighting the complementary nature of the components of internal control, the COSO Framework also emphasizes the need for these components to exist across all levels of an organization. In other words, the control environment, risk assessment, control activities, information and communication and monitoring must all exist at both entity and process levels. A strong board can establish an organization-wide culture of control and monitor controls at the top level, but in the absence of similarly tight controls lower down within the organization, the objectives may still not be achieved. There are strong parallels here with the budgeting process. A master budget may look good, but its achievement is potentially jeopardized by failure within a component such as the production or staffing budget.

The net result of an effective internal control system is a world of no surprises in which operational targets are achieved, financial reports are reliable and no penalties are incurred for non-compliance with laws and regulations.

COSO 1992 and Sarbanes-Oxley

Some commentators would argue that the COSO Framework simply documents the way in which well governed businesses organize their internal control systems, and does not contain any innovative thinking. Whilst this may be true, it does not negate the value of COSO in formally documenting a framework that can be used by less well managed organizations that seek to establish internal controls. Indeed Gupta (2006) comments that the COSO 1992 Framework consolidated the then fragmented thinking on internal control in one place, and suggests that its role in defining the principles of good internal control has stood the test of time. It is useful to review the rather limited evidence on the extent to which COSO 1992 was adopted by US companies in terms of two separate time periods – pre- and post-SOX. A 1996 survey of 300 senior executives and 200 non-management employees conducted by Coopers and Lybrand and cited by Gupta (2006) found very limited take-up of the COSO model, with only 10 per cent of executives saying they were aware of its existence (Kane et al., 1996). The implication is that 'COSO 1992 was more of a philosophical treatise written by a group of accountants to draw the attention of C suite executives to the concept of internal control as a fundamentally sound business practice' (Gupta, 2006, p. 59).

The picture that emerges in the post-SOX era is, however, fundamentally different. A recent report published by the Advisory Committee on smaller Public Companies (Washington, 2006, p. 23) revealed that the COSO 1992 Framework 'has emerged as the only internal control framework available in the US and the framework used by virtually all US companies.' The explanation for the change in usage between 1996 and 2006, and the resultant emergence of the COSO 1992 Framework as the dominant model for internal control design amongst US companies lies in the events that unfolded over the period 1992–2002, and most particularly the SOX.

The 1990s was characterized by a spate of corporate disasters and malfeasance represented by examples such as Healthsouth, WorldCom, Global Crossing and Enron that focused the attention of company executives on the consequences of ineffective internal controls. The SOX, signed by President Bush in 2002, was designed to help respond to these disasters by restoring investor confidence in financial reporting through the enactment of governance reforms and the establishment of the Public Company Accounting Oversight Board (PCAOB).

If it is accepted that SOX emerged in order to protect investors, shareholders and creditors from the breakdowns in internal control that result in financial disasters (Solomon and Peecher, 2004), then there is something of a sense of déjà vu in the perspective taken by SOX, because its objectives so clearly revisit the aims that underpinned the Foreign Corrupt Practices Act (FCPA) of 1977. SOX effectively affirmed that the FCPA had not been sufficiently effective in ensuring the reliability of public financial reporting and directly linked the reliability of financial statements to the maintenance of effective internal control systems.

One of the most widely debated provisions of SOX is Section 404. This requires that when a company registers its annual filing with the Securities and Exchange Commission (SEC), this should include an internal control report which:

- States management's responsibility for establishing and maintaining an adequate internal control structure and procedures for financial reporting; and
- Contains an assessment of the effectiveness of the company's internal control structure and procedures for financial reporting.

Gupta (2006) comments that the logic that underpins Section 404 is sensible and difficult to refute. Furthermore, he believes that the true intent of Congress in passing the legislation was to minimize the risk of 'materially wrong external audit opinions'. The argument is that reliable risk and control systems are likely to produce more reliable financial statements. This raises the issue of how control effectiveness can be assessed and the requirement for management to produce documentary support for their claims of effectiveness.

In June 2003 the SEC adopted rules on the implementation of Section 404 with regard to the management's obligations to report on its internal control structure. The regulations relating to the report on internal control structure are defined as follows:

- the evaluation must be based on procedures sufficient both to evaluate the design and to test the operating effectiveness of ICFR; and
- the assessment, including testing, must be supported by reasonable evidential matter.

The procedures that underpin the evaluation process effectively require that a suitable evaluation framework is specified and, whilst the SEC do not mandate the use of a single framework, they do indicate that the COSO 1992 guidelines provide an example of a 'suitable framework' (SEC, 2006, p. 5). In a footnote, the SEC also cite the Guidance on Assessing Control published by the Canadian Institute of Chartered Accountants (CoCo) and the report published by the Institute of Chartered Accountants in England & Wales Internal Control: Guidance for Directors on the Combined Code (known as the Turnbull Report) as examples of other suitable frameworks that issuers could choose in evaluating the effectiveness of their internal control over financial reporting.[1]

For US-based companies, or foreign companies with a US listing, the implication is clear: adopt the COSO Framework and you are likely to comply with Section 404. This explains why the COSO 1992 framework has become the dominant model for internal control design amongst US companies.

Before considering the suitability of the model for this purpose, it is helpful to look at how COSO responded to the financial crises of the 1990s and early years of the 21st century by revising their framework for internal control.

---

[1] It is important to note that the position of the SEC has now (2007) changed and the COSO model is no longer seen as adequate for use as an evaluation framework. This issue is discussed later in this chapter, and in much greater depth in Chapter 6.

COSO 2004: Enterprise risk management – Integrated framework

In 2004, COSO published a revised version of its internal control framework entitled Enterprise Risk Management – Integrated Framework (COSO, 2004). The revised framework added three additional components to the control framework, and it is useful to consider the extent to which this changed the internal control framework as proposed in the COSO 1992 report.

COSO 1992 defines internal control as being characterized as comprising five inter-related components. The five elements are as follows:

1. Control environment
2. Risk assessment
3. Control activities
4. Information and communication
5. Monitoring.

Under COSO 2004 three new components are added, namely:

- Objective setting
- Event identification, and
- Risk response.

At first glance the amendments appear relatively marginal, because the new components could be regarded simply as subsets of the risk assessment component in the 1992 version. The 2004 report argues, however, that the new framework 'expands on internal control, providing a more robust and extensive focus on the broader subject of enterprise risk management . . . that incorporates the internal control framework within it' (COSO 2004, Foreword, p. v). The very title of the document emphasizes what appears to be a shift in thinking which has the effect of raising the profile of risk management, as it is transformed from being a *component* of internal control to something which effectively *encompasses* internal control. This change in thinking is of great potential significance for the risk and audit professions.

The COSO document broadens the definition of risk, and emphasizes the value adding potential of risk management as a means of enhancing strategic decision making (Deloitte & Touche, 1997). The 2004 COSO Framework defines ERM as follows:

> Enterprise risk management is a process, effected by an entity's board of directors, management and other personnel, applied in strategy setting across the

enterprise, designed to identify potential events that may affect the entity, and manage risk to be within its risk appetite, to provide reasonable assurance regarding the achievement of entity objectives.

(COSO, 2004, p. 2)

Three fundamental entity objectives remain unchanged from the 1992 version of the Framework, namely:

1. Effectiveness and efficiency of operations
2. Reliability of financial reporting
3. Compliance with laws and regulations.

The 2004 Framework adds a fourth objective to the list at the strategic level. It states that ERM is geared to helping an entity achieve the high-level goals that support its overall mission. This serves to broaden the role of risk management to encompass all levels of the organization.

In summary, there are three key areas of difference between the 1992 and 2004 versions of the COSO Framework. Firstly, the 2004 Framework regards enterprise risk management as the factor critical to the achievement of organizational objectives, whereas the 1992 Framework sees internal control as the critical factor. Secondly, in managing risk within an enterprise, COSO 2004 specifies the need for risks to be assessed and managed within the context of the broader organizational objectives, which will in turn affect the selected response to any identified risk. Thirdly, COSO 2004 sees risk management as serving a strategic function.

In effect, the 2004 framework is redefining internal control in terms of risk management and potentially redrafting the lines of responsibility for internal control. It is noticeable that a new coordinating role is emerging in the form of the Chief Risk Officer, with responsibility for establishing and managing the systems for risk identification, monitoring and management across an organization. Dickinson (2001) names major companies such as Royal Bank of Canada, Charles Schwab and Ford Motors as among those choosing to appoint such an officer. This changing perspective on the significance of risk management opens up the possibility of the development of professional turf wars between the newly emerging profession of risk managers, staff within internal audit and operational management. Corporate culture will help determine which party ends up taking charge of the control process, but the new thinking implies that accountants may need to review their role as the designers and managers of financial controls.

How popular is ERM?

The broad perspective of risk management implied within ERM requires an organization to develop a very comprehensive strategy to identify, measure, monitor and control a vast array of risk exposures, and communicate its risk policies to staff at all levels via the creation of a risk aware culture. This is a very broad remit as it encompasses all hierarchical levels within the company as well as multiple functions, and hence poses major challenges in its practical implementation. Perhaps not surprisingly, therefore, there is some evidence to indicate a limited take-up of ERM to date.

Empirical research into the extent of adoption of ERM systems is made difficult by the fact that whilst the COSO Framework uses the specific term Enterprise Risk Management, it may be the case that companies are managing their risks in an integrated way but not using this terminology to describe their system. Furthermore, Enterprise Risk Management existed before COSO, and the term means slightly different things to different people. The result is that whilst a business may describe their system as 'holistic risk management', 'strategic risk management' or 'company-wide risk management' all of these may effectively equate to ERM.

In a survey of internal auditors, focused primarily on US-based companies, Beasley et al. (2005) found that only 48 per cent of the 174 respondents had at least a partial ERM system in place in their companies, and a further one-third were planning to implement ERM in the future. Beasley's findings need to be viewed with caution however, because the survey response rate was only 10 per cent, and the majority of respondents were from large US corporations with annual sales in excess of $1.3 billion. There is therefore a danger in generalizing up from such results, but they nonetheless offer some indications that the adoption of ERM is still in its relatively early stages.

A mail and telephone survey of members of the Canadian Risk and Insurance Management Society, published rather earlier in 2003, yielded very similar results. The researchers found that only 31 per cent of the sample had adopted ERM, although a larger proportion of companies were moving in that direction by developing guidelines for company-wide risk management (Kleffner et al., 2003). Interestingly, the propensity to use ERM did not appear to differ between those firms listed on the Toronto Stock Exchange and those not listed there, despite the fact that compliance with the exchange's guidelines requires ERM adoption.

It is difficult to speculate as to the reasons for the relatively slow adoption of ERM, but Kleffner et al. (2003) suggest that the major deterrents were organizational structure and a resistance to change. Furthermore, both the US and Canadian surveys were published quite early in the history of the development of ERM and it might be expected that the relative complexity of designing and instigating an ERM would take some time. Another possible explanation is that risk management systems within even the largest of organizations are still evolving, and the transformation from a silo-based methodology of risk management to a more holistic enterprise-based one is a tale of slow but steady evolution that is as yet incomplete. An additional possibility is that the fine distinction between risk and internal control that is made in the two COSO frameworks is less obvious in practice. In other words, companies may be engaged in ERM but regard the infrastructure that they use to do this as a broad governance and internal control framework rather than risk management. More cynically, it could even be argued that the mechanisms and procedures that characterize ERM are no different to those which could be found in any book on management control systems from 30 years ago. All that has changed is the language.

Consultants seeking to 'sell' the ERM approach talk of the 'value proposition of ERM', and suggest that adopters have found that whilst such a programme may require extensive management resources and take a number of years to complete, the benefits nevertheless outweigh the costs. Examples of adopters who have gained from ERM use include the Canadian Bank CIBC, which began a plan to introduce ERM in 1994. Lam (2006) argues that ERM enabled the bank to respond to early warning indicators that saved it from significant losses in the 1998 Russian currency crisis. From an academic perspective, the difficulty with such examples is that it is not easy to separately identify the factors that worked to reduce losses, as in the CIBC case. There may have been multiple interlinking factors at play and it is difficult to be categorical in attributing the benefit entirely to ERM. Nevertheless, it is incontestable that good internal control, governance and risk management are beneficial.

SOX Section 404 versus ERM

As already indicated, the SOX legislation was driven by a desire to improve the reliability of financial reporting, and a belief that good internal controls will serve to provide reasonable assurance of such reliability. The practical result of the legislation has been to focus attention on controls over financial reporting and this has been at the risk of potentially downgrading all of the other dimensions of internal control that contribute to good governance. The legislation has been criticized for focusing on too narrow a definition of risk, expressed purely in terms of the financial reporting process. If the consensus view is that ERM is the way to go, even if progress in this regard is still quite slow, then enacting legislation that redefines risk in purely reporting terms would appear to be a backward step.

The consequences of a shift in focus towards a concentration on financial reporting controls are two-fold, and offer an excellent example of the so-called law of unintended consequences. Firstly, at an internal level, they can lead to a diversion of corporate resources towards compliance efforts, which may jeopardize control practices in other areas of the business as well as diverting cash flow from potentially value-generating investments. There is growing evidence that small firms are suffering disproportionately from the high cost of creating compliance systems, and even the largest companies are complaining about the costs. SOX compliance is seen as a form of hidden taxation, but it may also be one which is economically inefficient. In a speech to the British Banking Association's Supervision Conference in 2006, Richard Gossage, the Head of Group Risk at the Royal Bank of Scotland cited research which estimated the total loss in market value from the major scandals such as Enron, WorldCom, Tyco and global Crossing at US $427 billion compared with estimated costs to companies of implementing SOX that amount to US $1.4 trillion. The numbers just do not add up and suggest that the legislation is not cost-effective.

Secondly, the high compliance costs can affect the attractiveness of the US markets to foreign listings. In a comment letter to the SEC, the US Chamber of Commerce argued that the Section 404 requirements had the potential to damage the long-term competitiveness of both US companies and the US capital markets. The attractiveness of Initial Public Offerings (IPO) in the US market is significantly reduced by the potential scale of the compliance burden, and in 2006 the Financial Times reported a speech by Alan Greenspan, the former head of the US Federal Reserve Bank in which he described himself as 'acutely aware and disturbed' (*Financial Times*, 2006) by the shift in IPOs away from the US and towards London as a consequence of SOX.

In response to a barrage of pressure about compliance costs, the SEC acknowledged a need to review its guidance on implementation of Section 404, and in May 2006 they arranged a roundtable discussion to obtain feedback from companies and audit firms on their experiences. Later that month, the SEC published 'Management's Report on Internal Control over Financial Reporting' (SEC, 2006) which contained interpretative guidance on completion of the annual control effectiveness report, as well as amendments to the initial rules on internal control over financial reporting that were laid down in June 2003 (see above).

In their 2006 report, the SEC reiterated the view that the evaluation methodology cannot be prescribed as circumstances will vary from company to company, but much more fundamentally, they revised their view of the COSO 1992 Framework in this regard. The SEC (SEC, 2006, p. 6) state that

> While the COSO framework identifies the components and objectives of an effective system of internal control, it does not set forth an approach for management to follow in evaluating the effectiveness of a company's Internal Controls over Financial Reporting (ICFR). We, therefore, distinguish between the COSO framework as a definition of what constitutes an effective system of internal control and guidance on how to evaluate ICFR for purposes of our rules.

This change of view significantly downgrades the importance of the COSO 1992 Framework as a point of reference for US public companies. The reasons for the change in the guidance are multiple, but Gupta (2006) suggests that one key factor may have been that companies and auditors were focusing on a bottom-up approach to assessment, rather than the top-down and more cost-effective way that was originally envisaged by the legislation. He concludes that the bottom-up approach results in a failure to focus on the real risks facing the business, which would suggest that Section 404 may still fail to prevent corporate disasters.

European Union regulations on risk and internal control certification

The European Directive on Statutory Audit concurs with the views of the Treadway Commission and US legislators in declaring that '. . . effective internal control systems contribute to minimize financial, operational and compliance risks and enhance the quality of financial reporting' (EU, 2006a, p. 87). Support for the principles of good internal controls does not, however, necessarily equate to support for prescribed control frameworks or legislative requirements such as SOX.

It would seem, in fact, that international convergence in the area of internal control certification is not on the horizon (Gupta, 2006). Amongst EU member countries, the Turnbull Review Group in the UK opted against requiring

SOX-style statements on internal control effectiveness, and at a Union-wide level, the European Corporate Governance Forum on Risk Management and Internal Control has responded to the debate about compliance costs re SOX by declaring a view that regulation and corporate governance codes need to be proportionate and that 'there is no need to introduce a legal obligation for boards to certify the effectiveness of control at EU level' (EU, 2006b). In addition, the Forum also recognizes a need to draw lessons from the recent risk management and internal control initiatives around the world, before introducing any further legislative measures. They recognize the need for further work on identifying best practices and a set of principles that can facilitate the implementation of effective control systems.

As yet, not all EU member states have a formal Corporate Governance Code, although all states are being encouraged to introduce one. There is encouragement for new codes to be drafted in accordance with the underlying principle of 'comply or explain' which has become a feature of Europe's approach to corporate governance. The European Corporate Governance Forum strongly supports this approach[2] which is justified on the basis of its flexibility to accommodate the requirements of different company situations as well as variations across national legal and governance frameworks, as discussed in Chapter 1. In terms of formal regulation, the principle is that the role is simply to verify the existence of the 'comply or explain' statement, and also to challenge any blatant misrepresentation of the facts. This means that any evaluation of the 'quality' of the statement should be left to shareholders and users of the annual report and financial statements. The principle does not preclude individual member states from imposing more detailed regulations if they so wish, particularly in relation to governance disclosures, but it sets a baseline for a common approach across Europe.

The European approach is thus fundamentally different to that of the US, where the Section 404 requirement for assessment of financial controls requires a judgement on control quality to be made by both management and external auditors. It remains to be seen whether or not these differences will persist over the longer term, or whether growing pressures from global capital markets, in combination with accounting harmonization, will lead to a global convergence of risk and internal control regulations.

---

[2] The full text of the forum's statement on 'comply or explain' can be found under http://ec.europa.eu/internal_market/company/ecgforum/index_en.htm

Conclusion

This chapter has sought to explain the background to the COSO Frameworks (1992 and 2004) on internal control and risk management, including a discussion of the reasons for the shift in thinking over the period 1992 to 2004. I have demonstrated that it is difficult to understand the significance of the COSO model without some associated understanding of the SOX (2002), which has itself been the subject of much criticism for the cost of compliance.

The picture that emerges is one in which there seem to be apparently conflicting forces at work in the world of risk and control. In the USA, for example, there is on the one hand the widely held view that effective internal control requires the implementation of ERM, which may take some years to complete. At the same time, there is a US-regulatory view that the primary consideration is financial controls that are essential to providing reassurance on the reliability of financial statements. This narrowing of the definition of risk appears to be in direct conflict with the culture of ERM. In Europe, the approach is one of trust via a 'comply or explain' approach to governance, rather than reliance upon auditors' assessment of internal control effectiveness. This principle is not currently universally applicable across Europe because of a need for some member states to introduce national governance codes.

It would therefore seem that approaches to guidance and regulation on risk and control are globally diverse, and the prospects for convergence are uncertain. The only firm point of agreement is that risk management and effective internal control are fundamental prerequisites of good corporate governance.

References

Beasley, M.S., Clune, R. and Hermanson, D. (2005). 'ERM: A Status Report', *The Internal Auditor*, Vol. 62, No. 1, pp. 67–73.

Committee of Sponsoring Organisations of the Treadway Commission (COSO) (1992). *Internal Control-Integrated Framework*, AICPA, New York, NY.

Committee of Sponsoring Organisations of the Treadway Commission (COSO) (2004). *Enterprise Risk Management-Integrated Framework*, AICPA, New York, NY.

Deloitte & Touche LLP (1997). *Perspectives on Risk*, Deloitte & Touche Tohmatsu International.

Dickinson, G. (2001). 'Enterprise Risk Management: Its Origins and Conceptual Foundation', *The Geneva Papers on Risk and Insurance*, Vol. 26, No. 3, pp. 360–366.

EU (2006a). Directive 2006/43/EC of the European Parliament and of the Council, 17 May.

EU (2006b). European Corporate Governance Forum, Annual Report 2006; Annex 3.

Financial Times (2006). 'Greenspan Predicts U.S. Governance Revamp'. 13 April, London.

Gupta, P. (2006). *COSO 1992 Control Framework and Management Reporting on Internal Control: Survey and Analysis of Implementation Practices*. IMA, Montvale, NJ.

Kleffner, A., Lee, R. and McGannon, B. (2003). 'The effect of corporate governance on the use of Enterprise Risk Management: Evidence from Canada', *Risk Management and Insurance Review*, Vol. 6, No. 1, pp. 53–73.

Krane, Drake and Sever (1996). *The Coopers & Lybrand Survey of Internal Control in Corporate America: A Report on What Corporations Are and Are Not Doing to Manage Risks*. Louis Harris & Associates, New York.

Lam, J. (2006). 'Managing risk across the enterprise: Challenges and Benefits', in Ong, M. (ed.), *Risk Management: A Modern Perspective, 1st edition*. Elsevier, Burlington, MA.

MaLave, N. (1996). 'Breakthrough Approaches to Managing Risk', *Bank Management*, March–April, pp. 1–10.

Nottingham, L. (1997). 'A conceptual framework for integrated risk management', Members' Briefing Publication 212–97, The Conference Board of Canada.

Securities and Exchange Commission (2006). 'Management's Report on Internal Control over Financial Reporting'. File number S7-24-06.

Selim, G. and McNamee, D. (1999). 'The Risk Management and Internal Auditing Relationship: Developing and Validating a Model', *International Journal of Auditing*, Vol. 3, pp. 159–174.

Shank, J. and Miguel, J.S. (2006). 'Merging financial and managerial accounting: strategic cost management and enterprise risk management under SOX'. Paper presented to MARG annual conference, London.

Solomon, I. and Peecher, M. (2004) 'SOX 404 – A Billion here, a billion there', *Wall Street Journal*, 9 November.

Unsworth, E. (1996). 'EU risk managers assume larger risk', *Business Insurance*, November, p. 13.

From Internal Auditing to Enterprise Risk Management: The Case of the Telecom Italia Group

Sergio Beretta* and Saverio Bozzolan†

*Bocconi University, Italy
†University of Padova, Italy

Introduction: Corporate governance, internal auditing and risk management

Risk management activities are primarily focused on how to ensure that top management runs the company in the interests of its stakeholders and in observance of the rules that regulate the competitive, economic, political and social environment (ICAEW, 1999). In the case of listed companies, the protection of investors' interests and the efficiency of financial markets are fundamental objectives.

The issuance of guidelines and codes of conduct reflecting best practices in Corporate Governance drafted by several national Committees (Cadbury, Greenbury, Hampel, UK 1992–1998; Turnbull, UK 1999–2005; Dey, Canada 1994; Vienot, France 1995–1999; Peters, Netherland, 1997; Cardon, Belgium 1998; Olivencia, Spain 1998; Preda, Italy 1999–2006) and professional bodies (CICA, 1995; ICAEW, 1999) prompted widespread re-consideration of the relationships linking internal control and risk management.

For example, in its guide to the implementation of the Dey Commission's report (1994) on communication to investors regarding the state of internal control systems, the Canadian Institute of Chartered Accountants (CICA, 1995) recommended that internal control systems include risk assessment and monitoring.

The Turnbull Report (FRC, 2005), which provides a framework for the implementation of a system of risk management for companies listed on the London Stock Exchange (LSE), encourages top management to explore the entire map of their companies' activities and resources, to identify the major risks to which their companies are exposed.

The Combined Code (FRC, 1999–2006; Stock et al., 1999) holds the directors of companies listed on the LSE responsible for the introduction of internal control systems designed to identify, control, monitor and communicate company risks.

The Italian Corporate Governance Code (Borsa Italiana, 1999–2006) holds the board of directors responsible for the effectiveness of internal control systems and requires that the main risks facing the company are identified and managed properly.

In other countries, the dissemination of risk management and related internal control systems has been driven by regulatory provisions. In Germany, the

'German Act on Corporate Control and Transparency' ('Gesetz zur Kontrolle und Transparenz im Unternehmensbereich – KonTraG', 1998) introduced an obligation for the Executive Committee to implement adequate risk management systems and appropriate internal auditing mechanisms (Luck, 1999).

Since the issuance of the COSO Report (COSO, 1992), the intensity of the ties between internal auditing and risk management has increased, as the role of internal auditing has evolved from inspection to risk assessment, thus offering assurance to management and to audit committees that business risks are clearly understood and effectively managed (IIA, 2002–2004; Allegrini and D'Onza, 2003; Gwilliam, 2003). Internal auditing supports the risk management process throughout the organisation by providing tools and techniques for the identification and the evaluation of business risks, by auditing the risk management process and by co-ordinating risk reporting to senior management (Chambers, 1993; IIA – UK and Ireland, 2002).

One of the most effective declarations of the close connections between internal control systems and risk management practices is found in the Turnbull Report, whereby 'Internal Control has as its principal aim the management of risks [...] We can assume that a company has effective internal controls if it has a rigorous corporate risk management system [...] A sound system of internal control is to be defined in terms of the policies and procedures that, taken together, enable the company to respond to significant risks.' (FRC, 1999).

Thus, generally speaking, according to the rules of corporate governance, internal control is closely related to risk management (IIA-UK, 1999; Messier, 2000; De Loach, 2000; Beretta and Bozzolan, 2004).

The change of a paradigm: From internal auditing to enterprise risk management

Practitioners have long considered risk assessment as an activity to be performed in the audit process with the specific aim to identify areas of weakness or symptoms of potential failure. Specifically, since the issuance of the COSO Internal Control Integrated Framework (IC-IF) (COSO, 1992), risk assessment is explicitly regarded as one of the components of internal control systems.

Nonetheless, the recent scandals and financial crashes that hit several large listed companies laid bare the inadequacy of internal control systems in directing management attention and resources towards risk management. An answer to the increasing demand for a more risk-focused perspective in the design and implementation of internal control systems has been given recently by COSO through the Enterprise Risk Management Integrated Framework (ERM-IF) (COSO, 2004).

This framework is a development of the previous IC-IF report (COSO, 1992). In the 1992 report, the identification and assessment of risk were considered strictly an aid in determining the adequacy of internal control systems. In fact, emphasis was placed on the internal control system, risk assessment being only one element of the control process. In the ERM framework, risk management is a key governance activity and internal control is an element of the ERM system. In order to appreciate its relevance and scope, risk management must be examined in connection with:

- Corporate governance, as top management is responsible for conscious and effective risk management;
- Performance measurement, as risk assessment is a key ingredient of risk-adjusted return measures;
- Internal control, as internal control is considered a component of Enterprise Risk Management systems.

Since it is defined as 'a process, effected by an entity's board of directors, management and other persons, applied in strategy setting and across the enterprise, designed to identify potential events that may affect the entity, and manage risks to be within its risk appetite, to provide reasonable assurance regarding the achievement of entity objectives' (COSO, 2004), ERM is closely linked to both strategy definition and strategy implementation. Thus, risk management is a process guided by the company's mission and strategic objectives, which unfolds along three phases:

1. *Risk identification*. Risks that may influence the achievement of company objectives and the success of company's strategies are pinpointed. Risks can be two-sided or downside. In the first case, once identified, they are channelled into the process of strategic planning. In the second case, they must be analysed thoroughly so that defence strategies may be devised. Interdependencies among different risk factors should be identified in order to neutralise dangerous concatenations or to properly manage common causal factors.

2. *Risk assessment.* The assessment of the identified risks makes it possible to appraise the impact of different risk factors on performance. The evaluation of these effects must be combined with an estimate of the probability of occurrence associated with these risk factors. Such combined assessment of impact and likelihood allows for a rational allocation of management attention to the different risk factors.

3. *Risk response.* Following the identification and the assessment of risks, management must act in order to implement risk management policies aimed at aligning the real risk profile to the one negotiated with shareholders.

The process of risk management is shaped by the internal environment, the control activities, the information and communication systems and the continuous monitoring of the system's adequacy.

The internal environment reflects the approach of management to risk governance. This environment is the result of a process through which top management recognises the risk implications of strategies, defines its risk appetite and encourages the desired risk tolerance within the enterprise.

Policies for risk control must be derived from these elements. These policies concern control activities and procedures and organisational solutions aimed at risk containment. In the ERM framework, information and communication systems play a dual role. On one side, by channelling information throughout the firm, they support effective decision-making and the efficient execution of strategies. On the other side, they are designed to make stakeholders and management aware of the risks that the enterprise is assuming. Continuous monitoring of the effectiveness of risk assessment procedures and the adequacy of control mechanisms is necessary, given the dynamics that affect both the competitive environment and the internal organisation.

In light of the above, an internal control process that effectively supports risk management must:

- be able to identify the risks threatening the business (McCuaig, 1998; De Loach, 2000);
- be integrated into the processes of strategic objectives setting and of strategic resources allocation (Lorange, 1980);
- be closely linked to the process of budgeting and assignment of objectives to management (Lawrie et al., 2003);
- ensure the continuous monitoring of risk management strategies (McNamee and Selim, 1998).

Figure 3.1 shows an internal control process with these features.

The starting point of the process is the identification of business risks, an activity driven by different elements and factors. On one side, risks emerge from the development of alternative scenarios of the environment (industries and countries) in which the firm operates (environmental risk factors). On the other side, performance measurement systems can act as potential generators of risks, as extremely challenging goals can lead to potentially risky organisational and managerial solutions. Moreover, an excessive rigidity in performance evaluation may induce undesirable behaviour in management (Simons, 1995). This seems to be the more so when incentive systems play a central role in

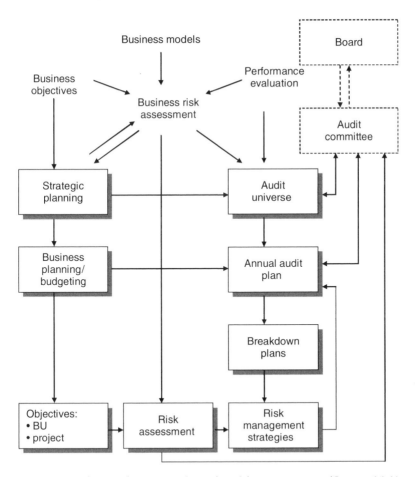

Figure 3.1 An internal control process oriented to risk management (*Source*: McNamee and Selim, 1998 [our elaboration])

driving management decisions and behaviour. It is one of the responsibilities of top management to check whether excessive pressure for results is prompting management to engage in moral hazard.

The process of internal control moves in parallel and in synchrony with strategic objectives setting and resource allocation to strategic programmes and initiatives (strategic planning) (Lorange, 1980). As strategic planning can substantially modify the risk profile of a business, an analysis of the business plan can provide useful indications to internal auditing on the elements worth monitoring (audit universe).

The subsequent incorporation of the strategic plan into the budget generates operational programmes (which guide management action); performance objectives (upon which management's commitment is sought); the allocation of resources to the operational units (for the implementation of approved programmes).

Thus, the contents of the budget can drive the formation of the annual auditing plan (Lawrie et al., 2003). The precise definition of budgeted objectives and programmes makes for a more detailed analysis, assessment and quantification of the risks previously identified (risk assessment) and a precise definition of the contents of the annual auditing plan (breakdown plans) (Selim and McNamee, 1999a).

In the proposed process, the relationships between internal control and risk management are clearly set in an integrated perspective. On one side, as both the planning process and the process of internal control are based on the identification of business risks, they must be conducted in an integrated way. This is made possible by the parallel development of the phases of both processes and by the continuous exchange of information regarding the business risk profile: the strategic planning process feeds the audit universe, while the budget process contributes to the definition of a detailed auditing plan. On the other side, continuous supervision by the Audit Committee over the internal control process must ensure that top management and line management share a common language and common frames of reference on risk management. In this way, the Audit Committee assumes a key role in the internal control process, as stated by corporate governance principles.

Internal control systems are therefore faced with a radical shift in paradigm, as they turn from compliance verification systems to risk control systems. Elements of this change of paradigm are presented in Table 3.1.

Table 3.1 Risk control: Old and new paradigm

	Old paradigm	New paradigm
Focus	On effectiveness of control mechanisms and on respect of procedures	On any type of risk that might compromise the achievement of company objectives: effectiveness-efficiency of operation; reliability of financial reporting; compliance with laws, rules and regulations.
Approach	– responsive – fragmented	– anticipatory, pro-active – integrated
Responsibility	Concentrated in staff units (Internal Auditing and Finance)	Diffused through line managers (Board of Directors, Internal Auditing, Managers at all levels)
Frequency	Periodic recurrent activity + occasional *ad hoc* activity	Continuous process

At the heart of the new paradigm: Control and risk self-assessment

In 1980, the Financial Executive Research Foundation published a study on the internal control systems of US companies (White, 1980). The research openly criticised the effectiveness of the traditional (and widespread) command and control model based upon the rigid assignment of predefined duties and specific objectives to employees and on close supervision and direct control of behaviours and results.

Due to its philosophical premises, this model of governance is responsible for dangerous illusions that have negatively influenced top management behaviour (Johnson, 1992), including, among others, the illusion of remote control and the illusion of learning at the top.

The illusion of remote control is the belief that the organisation can be governed from afar, through the forwarding of guidance signals (to indicate the desired behaviour) and of corrective signals (in answer to the real behaviour observed). This control archetype bases its expectations of effectiveness on two planning assumptions: first, the unconditional adherence of the employees to the values and objectives of the company; second, the possibility to manage complex organisations through simple algorithms that can easily be deployed throughout the system.

The illusion of learning at the top is the belief that top management has the best learning capabilities and opportunities because they can rapidly accumulate experience through frequency of replication and a variety of learning opportunities. The illusion is rooted in the assumption that the rationality of top management, supported by a flow of continuous and reliable information, is able to capture the whole complexity of operations. As a consequence, centralised decision-making is always a good move and investment in learning abilities at the operational level are unnecessary.

The diffusion of these illusions drove large companies towards strongly centralised governance models, even when the benefits expected were largely offset by the costs of the rigidity induced. Moreover, in recent times the importance of creating and developing learning abilities at the operational level has been supported by theory as well as by empirical evidence (Senge, 1995; Nonaka, 1994; Nonaka and Takeuchi, 1995). Consequently, the concept of empowerment has gained increasing currency. Empowerment does not imply, however, giving up control. On the contrary, it requires a reinforcement of guidance and control systems in order to manage the autonomic drives deriving from decentralisation (Kornbluh et al., 1987; Johnson, 1992; Belasco and Sayer, 1995). In this perspective, the effectiveness of internal control systems is measured not only by their ability to avoid undesired behaviour, but also by their ability to direct employees' creativity towards value generation, balancing autonomic drives and the need for unified governance (Simons, 1995). Thus, internal control systems can no longer be considered as inspective techniques. Their recognition as corporate governance mechanisms makes line management the owner of internal control systems, while specialists (like internal auditors) are the depositaries of control and certification methodologies.

This change in perspective validates and explains the increasing importance and diffusion of self-assessment practices in internal control.

Control Self-Assessment (CSA) is a process where auditors and management work cooperatively to set and evaluate standards for control through workshops and discussion (Jordan, 1995; IIA-UK, 1995–1997; Wade and Wynne, 1999). The application of CSA changes the focus of internal auditing from an ex post–ad hoc review activity made against management to a steering, interactive control activity made together with management (McCuaig, 1998).

CSA intends to promote the efficiency and effectiveness of internal control through management participation (Melville, 1999): at higher hierarchical levels, giving a risk management focus to the audit action; at the operational level, supporting the assessment and improvement of operating control mechanisms through workshops.

CSA can especially strengthen the effectiveness of internal auditing when traditional techniques prove ineffective, as is frequently the case in the assessment of the control environment or in the assessment of the efficiency of less structured control mechanisms.

Control and Risk Self-Assessment (CRSA) is a derivation of CSA. It is a process specifically focused on risk identification and assessment (Melville, 1999). Typically, CRSA changes the focus of an audit review from a structured, objective appraisal of an organisation's control systems, where internal auditors analyse and test transactions, to a workshop-based forum for discussion and understanding of strategic and business risks.

Management's active participation places at the auditors' disposal a wealth of direct knowledge of how the business model works and the organisation reacts. These elements of knowledge can direct the action of auditing towards those areas that are perceived as more critical and risky.

CRSA can support internal control activities both in guiding control efforts on the basis of preliminary risk assessments and in promoting management's self-certification procedures, as an instrument for documenting the state of business processes and the connected risks and control mechanisms.

In sum, given the increasing involvement of management in control activities, benefits can be obtained from its motivated participation: CRSA derives knowledge from participation. Meanwhile, commitment and motivation to risk management can be strengthened through CRSA initiatives.

CRSA does not have only positive aspects. In particular, high management involvement represents one of its most significant limitations, as it can compromise the objectivity of the assessment. In order to limit this risk, overlaps between CRSA processes and internal auditing activities must be reduced by carefully defining the purposes and contents of each, in order to promote integration without confusion of roles. For this reason, some companies have opted for a clear distinction between staff resources dedicated to internal auditing and those assigned to CRSA activities, even creating two separate teams with different responsibilities, tasks, skills and methodologies, both reporting to the Chief Internal Auditor.

Telecom Italia Group: The control and risk self-assessment project[1]

A brief presentation of the Telecom Italia Group

The Telecom Italia Group (TIG) is national leader in ICT, serving over 50 million people and 3 million firms in Italy, with more than 27 million fixed lines and more than 26 million mobile phone lines. Over 2 million regular clients buy internet services. TIG also operates in related sectors, such as data services, value added services, Internet and Media, Information Technology, IT Research and Innovation.

The Group is active in 19 countries in fixed and mobile telephony, with a strong presence in Europe, in the Mediterranean area and South America. The Group's consolidated revenue in 2003 amounted to approximately 30 billion euros. The employees at the end of 2003 were around 110 000.

In 2001, Olimpia S.p.A. (acting as the arm of Pirelli & C. S.p.A.) bought a controlling interest in Olivetti S.p.A., the majority shareholder of Telecom Italia. This event marked a turnover in top management and a significant review of the Group's development strategies.

From the very beginning, the new board stated its intention to pay greater attention to corporate governance. TIG has adhered to the principles of corporate governance set out by Borsa Italiana S.p.A. and is included in the Dow Jones Sustainability Index.

The internal control system and the function of internal audit

In TIG's view, the Company's internal control system is a process designed to ensure: the efficiency of the management of corporate affairs and operations; the measurability and verifiability of this efficiency; the reliability of accounting and management data; compliance with all applicable laws and regulations

---

[1] Information and data concerning the Telecom Italia Group are referred to year 2003, when the CRSA project analysed in this paper was carried out. Authors wish to thank Mr Armando Focaroli and Mr Alberto Ragazzini (TIG) for their support.

whatever their origin; and the safeguarding of the Company's assets, inter alia so as to prevent fraud at its own and the financial market's expense (Telecom Italia Group, 2003: Art. 11).

Among the general principles accepted:

- the organisation's objectives must be clearly defined and adequately communicated to all the levels concerned;
- the risks associated with the achievement of objectives shall be identified and systematically monitored, and communicated to the corporate top management.
- Adverse events able to threaten the continuity of the organisation's operations must be subject to special evaluation and the related defence strengthened;
- the internal control system must be subject, in addition to continuous supervision by the Internal Control Committee, to periodic evaluations (Telecom Italia Group, 2003: Art. 11).

Within this framework, Internal Audit ensures the quality of the audit activities by verifying the adequacy of the internal control systems of both Group companies and Business Units, and the coordination of external audit activities. It operates on control, risk management and corporate governance processes.

Control and risk self-assessment in the Telecom Italia Group

The implementation of a control and risk self-assessment (CRSA) system originated from the board's wish to adhere to the best international standards of internal control and corporate governance. The second objective was to make CRSA a management tool designed to reinforce a control culture and promote a systematic assessment of business risks.

In order to ensure an effective implementation of the project, a supporting structure was established. There were three key bodies:

1. A Steering Committee, composed of top managers of the TI Group (BU Vice Presidents, CFOs, Chief Internal Auditor), acted both as project sponsor and supervisor by defining its strategic goals and monitoring its progress.

2. A Project Office, staffed with people from the Internal Audit department, was responsible for the definition of methodologies, coordination and management support during the project.
3. CRSA Points Of Reference, one for each business unit, which reported to the top management of their unit on the proper and effective application of the CRSA methodology.

Nonetheless, the choice to adopt a participatory approach to the implementation of CRSA gave management a central role in the execution of the initiative. The implementation of the project saw the active involvement of more than 500 managers (Table 3.2).

Management, in particular, was given the responsibility to identify and assess risks, to analyse the existing controls and to define and implement action plans to improve them.

Table 3.2 The CRSA project in the Telecom Italia Group: Managerial resources applied

	Hours	People involved
Purchasing	109	19
Human resources	76	18
Finance	59	34
Brand enrichment	37	11
IT	42	12
Public & economic affairs	84	18
TI-LAB	68	17
Corporate & legal affairs	63	13
Investor relations	26	9
La 7 (TV channel)	18	12
Virgilio – Tin.it (Internet)	34	11
TIM	795	137
TI-Wireline	447	140
Latin America	369	113
Total: Line Management	**2227**	**564**
TI – Project office	5622	6
Steering committee	209	5
Total	**8058**	**575**

The CRSA Project[2]

The CRSA project consisted of 7 phases: kick-off meeting; risk identification, risk consolidation; risk assessment; screening of significant risks; analysis of existing controls; closing workshop.

Kick-off meeting. The project started with a series of meetings with representatives from the Steering Committee, the components of the Project Office and first-level managers from corporate functions and business units (BU). These meetings had two objectives. The first was the presentation of the project, its philosophy and its role within TIG's corporate governance. The second was the illustration of the methodology, the resources involved and the time schedule of the project. Before the start of the project, TIG's top management fostered the creation of an internal environment favourable to risk management through a clear definition of:

- mechanisms of allocation of functional authority reflecting the risks connected to different types of operations;
- design criteria of organisational structures in order to avoid the concentration of decision-making powers in a single person without adequate control mechanisms (especially for those activities involving high risks);
- criteria of selection and management of human resources consistent with the ethical values and objectives determined by the company (Telecom Italia Group, 2003: Art. 11).[3]

Risk Identification. Management carried out this task by analysing relationships among objectives, resources and risks. The analysis was conducted both at the corporate level (functions) and at business unit level, in order to promote a critical comparison of the two perspectives in risk identification and risk assessment. The units' strategic objectives were deployed into specific and measurable sub-objectives. The critical success factors and the operational processes connected to each sub-objective, as well as the critical resources related to each operational process, were identified and analysed.

---

[2] The analysis of the CRSA experience is the result of the Authors' participation in the CRSA project. This participation included systematic meetings with members of the Project Office, attendance at the CRSA workshops and interviews with BU management and corporate staffs.

[3] These activities reflect the creation of a favourable *internal environment* as stated in the COSO ERM framework: 'Management sets a philosophy regarding risk and establishes a risk appetite. Environment sets the foundation for how risk and control are viewed and addressed by an entity's people. The core of any business is its people – their individual attributes, including integrity, ethical values and competence – and the environment in which they operate. They are the engine that drives the entity and the foundation on which everything rests' (COSO, 2003, p. 19).

It was decided not to distribute predefined lists of risks, nor to impose a constricted terminology for their evaluation. The choice to leave management utterly free was meant to elicit the full benefit of its wealth of knowledge and ideas. An association of the risk recognition activity with the identification of the relevant causal factors was strongly recommended, in order to reinforce the search for risk management solutions. Each operational unit identified a high number of risks: from a minimum of 10 to a maximum of 470 per unit, with an average of 180 risks identified. Special emphasis was placed on the identification of causal factors for each risk. The project office supported management in the application of risk identification methodologies, acting as a consultant.[4]

Risk consolidation. The high variety of risks identified by the business units prompted a significant effort by the project office to standardise the terminology used by the different units. Through continuous interaction with operating managers, the project office, acting as a consultant on risk assessment methodologies, could acquire a thorough understanding of the approach followed by each unit. This knowledge was paramount in the analysis and consolidation of the risk identification schedules prepared by local units.

All the risks identified by the operating units were then classified by type of risky event and by cause. With regard to the former, a traditional classification was adopted: external risks, process risks and information for decision-making risks. With regard to the second classification, causes were grouped according to their nature and genesis: organisation and human resources; availability of economic/financial resources; inefficiency of operational processes; strategic aspects.

The output of this phase was a list of consolidated risks, expressed using a uniform terminology and classified as proposed above. This led to a substantial reduction in the number of risk species assessed: from a minimum of 10 to a maximum of 82 per unit, with an average of 39 risks.

---

[4] This phase was intended to satisfy the *event identification* requirements of the COSO ERM framework: 'Potential events that might have an impact on the entity must be identified. Event identification includes identifying factors – internal and external – that influence how potential events may affect strategy and objectives. It includes distinguishing between potential events that represent risks, those representing opportunities and those that may be both. Management identifies the precipitating events, or root causes, of potential events, as a means of categorizing risks, which creates and reinforces a common risk language across an entity. It also provides a classification useful in recognizing interrelationships of potential events and a basis for aggregating or otherwise considering risks in a portfolio view' (COSO, 2003, p. 19).

Risk assessment. Managers of business units were required to assess the con-solidated risks according to their estimated impact and expected likelihood of occurrence (Table 3.3).

Due to the complexity of the business, it was thought that the appraisal of risks could benefit from the adoption of multiple perspectives. Accordingly, risks were assessed simultaneously by managers located both in the business units and at the corporate level. The disparity of judgements expressed by different people with regard to the same risk is a very important element of knowledge, as systematic diversities of opinion could alternatively signal inappropriate applications of the chosen investigation methods or misalignment in the per-ception of risks by managers. The distance in judgements is measured by the standard deviation of the distribution of both impact and probability. Figure 3.2 provides an example of risk metrics representing assessment deviations.

As it is clear from Figure 3.2 (the size of the disk that represents each risk indicates the extent of the deviation in judgement), the distribution of risks is heavily dependant on the organisational position of the respondent units. In particular, corporate managers show a greater propensity to more severe

Table 3.3 The CRSA project in Telecom Italia group: Risk classification grid

Value	Risk
Value ≥ .12	High
8 ≤ Value < 12	Medium
Value < 8	Low

Probability → Impact ↓	Low probability (1)	Medium probability (2)/(3)/(4)		High probability (5)
Extreme (5)				
Relevant (4)				
Medium (3)				
Scarce (2)				
Marginal (1)				

Source: Our elaboration based on internal documents of Telecom Italia Group

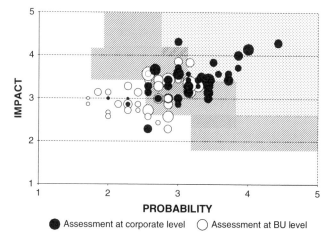

Figure 3.2 The CRSA project in Telecom Italia group: Risk mapping (*Source*: Our elaboration based on internal documents of Telecom Italia group (the proposed risk map does not represent the real situation))

judgements than managers located in business units and directly involved in the operations. The deviation can have two components: one physiological, the other pathological. The physiological component is in the influence determined by the distance from the business: whoever operates in close contact with the business has a natural association with operating risks, and therefore a greater risk tolerance than someone who looks at the business from afar. The pathological component is in the eventual misalignment of risk perception of line managers with the firm's risk management policies.

Most severe risks and risks characterised by large deviations in judgement were the focus of special attention and thorough debate in workshops.[5]

Screening of significant risks. In order to focus management's attention and workshop debate on a limited number of risks, and then build the relevant action plans, the project office ranked risks by impact and probability of occurrence. The most severe risks had to undergo a thorough analysis of causes, and existing controls had to be evaluated. Existing countermeasures and safeguards were evaluated to estimate residual risks.

---

[5] In the COSO ERM framework, the *risk assessment phase* consists in the analysis of identified risks 'in order to form a basis for determining how they should be managed. Risks are associated with related objectives that may be affected. Risk is assessed on both an inherent and a residual basis, and the assessment considers both risk likelihood and impact. There may be a range of possible results associated with a potential event, and management needs to consider them together' (COSO, 2003, p. 19).

Analysis of existing controls. Management (at corporate and in business units) and the project office jointly identified existing controls for selected risks in the light of the COSO framework. For each such risk, existing countermeasures and safeguards were identified and assessed.[6] If the assessment revealed inadequacies, plans of action would be defined in order to control, reduce or eliminate residual risks, according to the risk tolerance policy.

Closing workshop. A workshop, arranged at the end of the CRSA process, provided the opportunity for debate and discussion over the action plans proposed by line managers. During the workshop, guidelines were defined for action planning, providing guidance for the ensuing activities, the identification of the managers in charge and the time frame of the execution, as well as a summary evaluation of the costs and benefits of each action.[7]

In order to transform CRSA from an occasional activity into a continuous managerial practice, it would be necessary to maintain pressure on the process. To this end, four lines of action were undertaken:

1. the appointment of a CRSA Point Of Reference for each business unit, which would report to the unit's top management on the proper and effective application of the CRSA methodology;
2. the definition of rules and procedures for risk control that set out common practices and checkpoints aligned with the Group's risk governance strategy;
3. the creation of a permanent role of methodological support (selected from within the project office), to give continuity to the CRSA and to improve the methodology;
4. the implementation of an Action Plan Monitoring system.

Telecom Italia Group: Beyond and after internal auditing

Action plan monitoring

Extensive involvement of management in risk assessment and in the definition of audit action plans is a key mark of the TIG risk governance model.

---

[6] This phase corresponds to the *risk response* in the COSO ERM framework where 'Management selects an approach or set of actions to align the level of perceived risk with the entity's risk appetite, in context of the strategy and objectives. Personnel identify and evaluate possible responses to risk, including avoiding, accepting, reducing and sharing risk' (COSO, 2003, p. 19).

[7] These 'policies and procedures are established and executed to help ensure that risk responses are effectively carried out' (COSO, 2003, p. 19).

Nonetheless, the pressure on management to perform gave rise to an execution risk for these plans, thus compromising the effectiveness of the whole risk management process.

As a result, two factors were identified – management involvement and support structures and systems – which could give added impetus to the execution of the approved audit action plans.

Thus, on one side, responsibility for carrying out the plans was given, in addition to the managers in charge, to certain top managers who would report directly to the CEO/Board of Directors on the implementation of the audit action plans (hereinafter referred to as Audit Plan Supervisors).

On the other side, compliance managers were appointed and an Action Plan Monitoring System (APMS) was installed to help the audit plan supervisors to fulfil their mandates.

The audit plan supervisor and the compliance managers

The Audit Plan Supervisor is a key figure in the Telecom Italia Group's corporate governance system. Provisions are made for this position in Telecom Italia's Code on Corporate Governance (referred to by TI as Self-Regulatory Code), where responsibility for the proper functioning of the internal control system is assigned to a director who, in turn, may appoint one or more 'persons in charge of implementation' (i.e. Audit Plan Supervisors).

Audit Plan Supervisors are selected from among highly visible and reputable managers. They are given the task to monitor the progress of the audit action plans. Their role is to prod and support the managers of the different plans, as well as to report to the Group's Internal Control Manager on the milestones of the audit action plans, highlighting any failures and significant implementation criticalities.

Thus, Audit Plan Supervisors must fulfil such professional requisites as allow them 'to establish and maintain a system to monitor the disposition of results communicated to management' (standard 2500). The Chief Internal Audit Officer, instead, is responsible for the implementation of follow-up activities, and reports to the Audit Committee on the state of the control system as a whole.

Thus, Audit Plan Supervisors are faced with a major task, to be carried out along with their day-to-day duties. Audit Plan Supervisors play a proactive role thanks also to a dedicated staff made up of Compliance Managers, who are typically professionals with significant internal auditing experience and expertise.

Compliance Managers are responsible for encouraging line manager to execute the audit action plans and for the dissemination of a culture of governance and control methodologies. Thus, Compliance Managers fulfil the permanent role of methodological support mentioned above.

The action plan monitoring system

One of the operational criticalities of the monitoring activities performed in such a complex and far-reaching organisation as the Telecom Italia Group lies in the large number and variety of action plans under way in the different business units. The success of the monitoring activities depends largely on the availability of real-time information on the progress and milestones of the different plans. In order to provide Audit Plan Supervisors and Compliance Managers with the operational support necessary to receive such information, an Action Plan Monitoring (APM) software application was developed within the Group, which handles communications with the action plan managers and makes it possible to monitor progress vis-à-vis the action plans.[8] In keeping with the proactive approach to control fostered by Telecom Italia, with the introduction of APM, progress against the schedules set for each business unit is no longer updated by the Internal Auditing staff but by the action plan managers (Action Plan Implementation Manager and Action Development Manager).

APM is a web-based application, resident on the Group's intranet, accessible by area of responsibility to all the players involved in the process to improve the internal control system in Italy and abroad (Europe and Latin America) (Figure 3.3).

As usual, software applications can be used simply to automate existing processes or to implement change and improvement. In the case of APM, the introduction of the application has resulted in an improvement of the quality

---

[8] The APM application aims at fostering the flow of communication and significant information throughout the firm, as required by the COSO framework, 'in a form and timeframe that enable people to carry out their responsibilities. Information is needed at all levels of an entity for identifying, assessing and responding to risk. Effective communication also must occur in a broader sense, flowing down, across and up the entity. Personnel need to receive clear communications regarding their role and responsibilities' (COSO, 2003, p. 19).

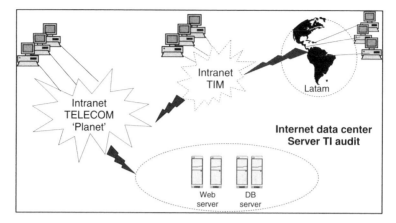

Figure 3.3 The Telecom Italia Group intranet architecture

of the action plans. In fact, in order to be utilised to feed the APM system, action plans must be:

- Adequately structured – each suggestion must entail implementation commitments, in terms of improvement, timing and accountability for every step taken by individual participants in all action plans.
- Placed in the hierarchy of organisational responsibilities – accountability must be traceable along the hierarchy, from the Implementation Manager, who oversees the individual participants, to the top levels (Corporate and Business Unit Managers; Subsidiaries' CEOs), so as to ensure adequate commitment both when plans are defined and when they are implemented.

The progressive dissemination of the APM system has shifted the focus of attention of the audit reporting system, from the production of documentary evidence on the status of the systems (control system diagnostics through Flash and Audit Reports) to plans to improve the system (Action Planning).

Profiles and roles of APM users

Consistent with the organisational design of the action plan system, APM calls basically for three user profiles:

1. *System administrator.* Responsible for the 'publication' of official action plans, the assignment of user roles and the handling of access credentials.

2. *User.* Responsible for managing and viewing the action plans falling under own responsibility. Based on the role assigned at the time the action plan was defined, there are three types of user:

- Audit Plan Supervisor – user responsible for monitoring the audit plan, analysing the state of implementation of suggestions, encouraging implementation progress, and reporting.
- Action Plan Implementation Manager – user responsible for approving the progress of corrective actions (rescheduling and status changes).
- Action Development Manager – user responsible for the structured entry of progress of the corrective actions.

3. *Reviewer.* User responsible for the overview of the implementation status of all the action plans entered into the system, as a support in follow-up activities.

Progress management and monitoring

For all action plans published, the APM system works as a schedule, until all the planned activities contained therein are fully implemented (Figure 3.4).

This application includes a control mechanism whereby the Action Development Manager is notified automatically 10 days prior to the completion dates of the planned activities. The lack of entries indicating progress in view of an upcoming deadline triggers a notification escalation process, involving the activation of follow-up notices by the Action Plan Implementation Manager and the Audit Plan Supervisor.

Thus, the persons responsible for the planned activities – promptly notified by the system as explained above – must update the progress report (possibly attaching the supporting documents in an electronic format), propose a status change in case they have been completed (Implemented, Cancelled) or recommend, specifying the grounds, a new completion date, if the original deadline cannot be met.

The proposals by the person responsible for planned activities, submitted when a 'status change' (action implemented or action cancelled) or a 'rescheduling' of completion dates is entered, are notified automatically for approval to the Action Plan Implementation Manager. In case of rejection, the system re-submits the schedule of the planned activities in question to the Action Development Manager.

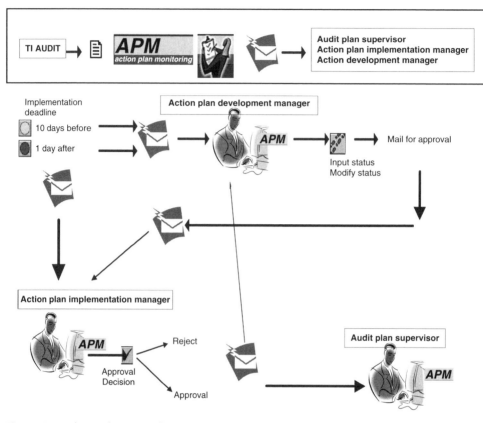

Figure 3.4 The Telecom Italia Group APM system (*Source*: Our elaboration of TIG documents)

The APM system has a reporting section which, thanks to different degrees of visibility by user type, makes it possible to aggregate the information entered analytically into the system.

The system generates customisable online reports based on the list of Action Plans, statistical reports on the percentage of completion of the planned activities designed also to control any rescheduling, and specific datasets for the periodic reporting of action plan progress by the Audit Supervisor Plan.[9]

---

[9] The APM application supports the *monitoring phase* as requested by the COSO framework, which states: 'The entire process must be monitored, and modifications made as necessary. In this way, the system can react dynamically, changing as conditions warrant. Monitoring is accomplished through ongoing management activities, separate evaluations of the enterprise risk management processes, or a combination of the two' (COSO, 2003, p. 19).

Conclusion: Lessons learned

The analysis of the TIG case bears out some of the insights that emerged from previous research and surveys on the relationship between internal control and risk management (Tillinghast Towers Perrin, 2001; IIA-UK 2002).

First, management's participation in, and commitment to, risk and control assessment allow for a better understanding of the strategic dimension and genesis of business risks. In TIG's experience, CRSA proved effective in bringing management closer to a culture of conscious control and management of risk.

Second, CRSA promotes the improvement of management skills and practices. In TIG's management judgement, the CRSA initiative has positively impacted risk management and internal control practices, internal auditors' skills and management control systems.

With regard to the first area, CRSA proved to be an effective tool in directing management attention towards risk management and corporate governance (Melville, 1999). In the case of TIG, CRSA has provided the managers of Business Units and the Group's top management with a clear view of the real sensibility of line management to the governance of risk and has created favourable conditions to perform accurate checks of the effectiveness and efficiency of existing controls. In top management's opinion,[10] CRSA

- has offered a realistic measure of the level of diffusion of a control culture and a clear perspective of the control environment, in view of the achievement of strategic objectives;
- has made management more aware of its responsibility for control activities and has facilitated the identification of strategic interdependencies between units and/or functions, which is important for the definition of the company's risk profile;
- has introduced the systematic production of documents supporting management reporting to the board of directors on internal control and risk management.

---

[10] The reported judgements have been gathered by the Authors:
- in a series of interviews with the top management of TIG (Chief Internal Auditing Officer; Planning and Control Systems Director; Risk Management Officer);
- during CRSA workshops to which they participated as listeners (Business Unit Directors and management; Corporate Functions Directors and management).

The practice of CRSA has offered a pragmatic, but not trivial, view of the genesis and governance of risks that can compromise the achievement of company objectives. Moreover, the activity of risk identification, which starts from the Group and business units' strategic objectives, has helped to promote the search for greater consistency in the process to allocate resources between the Group's strategic goals and management's short-term objectives.

With regard to the second area, previous research (Selim and McNamee, 1999b) offered empirical evidence on the enabling role of CRSA in promoting effective communication between the internal auditing staff and the rest of the organisation. As far as TIG is concerned, CRSA has positively impacted the development of cooperative relationships between internal auditors and line managers. The facilitating role played by the project office has encouraged the improvement (and, in some cases, the development) of interaction skills that the traditional profile of the Internal Auditor usually does not require. These skills involve the ability of interfacing with management, of managing the Group's dynamics and of constructively handling conflicts. Benefits are also expected in terms of both efficiency and effectiveness of internal auditing as the CRSA approach:

- Increases significantly the spectrum of the assessment activities that the internal auditing staff can manage by itself.
- Facilitates internal audits in areas that are usually poorly analysed because of the relevance of the managerial judgement component in the assessment, but whose impact on the risk profile of the Group is constantly increasing (including such new areas of risk as customer relationship management, quality systems, resource productivity improvement systems and so on).
- Fosters a more effective allocation of internal auditing resources by adopting a risk focused approach to the definition of the audit plan.
- Promotes a more effective communication to the Audit Committee on the company's risk profile and the state of internal controls.

With regard to the third area, the application of CRSA is changing the focus of internal auditing from an ex post–ad hoc review activity to continuous monitoring of risks and controls, based upon continuous interaction and collaboration between auditors and management (McCuaig, 1998). This change of focus within TIG is testified not only by the commitment of line management to the CRSA project, but also by the decision of top management to fully integrate the CRSA methodology into the planning and control process. To this end, responsibility for the systematic application of the CRSA methodology has been transferred to the Group's Finance and Control Department, and risk assessment has been integrated into the Group's planning, budgeting and reporting processes.

A third aspect has to do with the impact that internal auditing has on performance improvement: effectiveness of internal control lies in the rate of transformation of audit warnings into implemented action plans. This requires a change in the role of internal auditing, from inspection to facilitation, that does not involve only the attitudes and skills of internal auditors, but requires the creation of supporting mechanisms, too. TIG's creation of an Internal Control Manager role as well as its development of the APM system have been crucial to the re-focusing of internal auditing from ex post control to proactive risk management. Specifically, the support offered by the APM system in monitoring and reporting the status of action plans has proved the key both in feeding the Audit Committee with a continuous flow of information and in enlisting top management in the internal auditing activity. The direct supervision of top management is a strong incentive for the managers in charge to implement action plans effectively and accurately.

In conclusion, TIG's case shows the importance of involving management and generating its commitment, to spread a culture of conscious control and risk management. The role played by the internal auditing staff proved critical for the success of the CRSA initiative, in terms of both project coordination and support to management. Consistent with the strategic choice made by TIG's top management, the approach adopted encouraged management's maximum participation both in risk and control assessment and in the definition of action plans to be implemented to improve the system of controls. In order to fully appreciate operational management's cognitive and experiential contribution, debates and local studies have been promoted, offering methodological support where necessary.

Internal auditing has acted as a facilitator, sometimes sacrificing efficiency for the sake of effectiveness. By doing that, on one side risk assessment and control have started to be accepted as basic components of management decisions and actions. On the other side, management's appreciation of the input of internal auditing into the value creation process has increased dramatically.

References

Allegrini, M., D'Onza, G. (2003). 'Internal Auditing and Risk Assessment in large Italian companies: An Empirical Survey', *International Journal of Auditing*, Vol. 7, No. 3, 191–208.

Belasco, J.A., Sayer, R.C. (1995). 'Why Empowerment Doesn't Empower: The Bankrupt of Current Paradigms, *Business Horizons*, March–April, pp. 29–41.

Beretta, S. (2004). *Valutazione dei rischio e controllo interno*. Università Bocconi Editore, Milano.

Beretta, S., Bozzolan, S. (2004). 'A Framework for the analysis of firm risk communication', *The International Journal of Accounting*, Vol. 39, 265–288.

Borsa Italiana (1999–2006). Codice di Autodisciplina, Comitato per la Corporate Governance delle Società Quotate, Milano.

Chambers, A. (1993). *Effective Internal Audit*, Pitman, London.

Canadian Institute of Chartered Accountants (CICA) (1995). Guidance for Directors. Governance Processes for Control, Toronto (www.cica.ca).

Committee of Sponsoring Organizations of the Treadway Commission (COSO) (1992). *Internal Control-Integrated Framework*, AICPA New York, NY.

Committee of Sponsoring Organizations of the Treadway Commission (COSO) (2003). Enterprise Risk Management, Conceptual Framework, *Consultation Draft*, AICPA (www.coso.org).

Committee of Sponsoring Organizations of the Treadway Commission (COSO) (2004). *Enterprise Risk Management Integrated Framework*, AICPA New York, NY.

DeLoach, J.W. (2000). Enterprise-wide Risk Management, *Financial Times*, – Prentice Hall, London.

Financial Reporting Council (1999–2005). *Internal Control: Guidance for Directors on the Combined Code*, London.

Financial Reporting Council (1999–2005). The Combined Code on Corporate Governance, London.

Gwilliam, D. (2003). 'Audit Methodology, Risk Management and Non Audit Services: What Can We Learn From the Recent Past and What Lies Ahead', *Briefing 05.03*. Centre for Business Performance, ICAEW, London.

KPMG (1999). *Internal Control: A Practical Guide*. London, October.

Institute of Chartered Accountants of England and Wales (ICAEW) (1999). *Implementing Turnbull Report*, London, June (www.icaew.co.uk).

Institute of Chartered Accountants of England and Wales (ICAEW) (2000). *Risk management and the value added by Internal Audit*, London (www.icaew.co.uk).

Institute of Internal Auditors UK (IIA-UK) (1995). *Control Self Assessment and Internal Audit*, London (www.iia.org.uk).

Institute of Internal Auditors UK (IIA-UK) (1997). *Control Self Assessment and Internal Audit*, PBN 7, London.

Institute of Internal Auditors UK (IIA-UK) (1999). *Effective Governance*, London (www.iia.org.uk).

Institute of Internal Auditors UK (IIA-UK) (2002). *The Role of Internal Audit in Risk Management*, Position Statement (www.iia.org.uk).

Institute of Internal Auditors UK (IIA-UK) (2002). *Professional Practice Framework* (The standards for the Professional Practice of Internal Auditing), London.

Institute of Internal Auditors (IIA) (2004). *The Role of Internal Audit in ERM*, Position Statement (www.iia.org).

Kornbluh, H., Pipan, R., and Schurman, S.J. (1987). 'Empowerment, learning and control in workplaces', *Zeitschrift für Sozialisationforschung und Etziehungssoziologie*, Vol. 7, pp. 253–268.

Johnson, H.T. (1992). *Relevance Regained. From Top-Down Control to Bottom-Up Empowerment*. The Free Press, New York.

Jordan, G. (1995). *Control self assessment: Making the right choice*, The Institute of Internal Auditors Florida, USA.

Lorange, P (1980). Corporate Planning. *An Executive Viewpoint*, Prentice Hall – Englewood Cliffs, NJ.

Lawrie, G.J.G., Kalff, D.C. and Andersen, H.V. (2003). *Integrated Risk Management with Existing Methods of Strategic Control: Avoiding Duplication within the Corporate Governance Agenda*.

Presented at 6th International Conference on Corporate Governance and Board Leadership, Henley Management College, August.

Luck, W. (1999). *Betriebswirtschaftliche Aspekte der Einrichtung eines Überwachungssystems und eines Risikomanagementsystems*, Schäffer-Poeschel, Stuttgart.

McCuaig, B. (1998). Audit, assurance and Csa, *The Internal Auditor*, June, pp. 43–48.

McNamee, D. and Selim, G.M. (1998). *Risk Management: Changing the Internal Auditor's Paradigm*. The Institute of Internal Auditors Research Foundation, Altamonte Springs, FL.

Melville, R. (1999). 'Control Self Assessment in the 1990's: The UK Perspective', *International Journal of Auditing*, Vol. 3, No. 3, pp. 191–206.

Messier, W.F. Jr (2000). *Auditing*. McGraw Hill, Englewood Cliffs.

Nonaka, I. (1994). 'A Dynamic Theory of Organisational Knowledge', *Organisational Science*, Vol. 5.

Nonaka, I. Takeuchi, H. (1995). *The Knowledge Creating Company*. Oxford University Press, New York.

Selim, G.M. and McNamee, D. (1999a). The Risk Management and Internal Auditing relationship: What Are the Essential Building Blocks for a Successful Paradigm Change? *International Journal of Auditing*, Vol. 3, No. 2, pp. 147–155.

Selim, G.M. and McNamee, D. (1999b). 'The Risk Management and Internal Auditing relationship: Developing and Validating a Model', *International Journal of Auditing*, Vol. 3, No. 3, pp. 159–174.

Senge, P.M. (1995). *The Fifth Discipline. The art and practice of learning organisation*, Doubleday Currency, New York.

Simons, R. (1995). *Levers of Control*. Harvard Business School Press, Boston, MA.

Stock, M., Copnell, T. and Wicks, C. (1999). *The Combined Code. A Practical Guide*, GEE, London.

Telecom Italia Group (2003). Code of Conduct, October (www.telecomitalia.it).

Tillinghast Towers Perrin (2001). *Enterprise Risk Management: Trends and Emerging Practices*, The Institute of Internal Auditors Research Foundation, Altamonte Springs, FL.

Wade, K. and Wynne, A. (1999). *Control Self Assessment for Risk Management and Other Practical Applications*. Wiley and Sons, New York.

White, B.J. (1980). *Internal Control in US Corporations*. Financial Executive Research Foundation, New York.

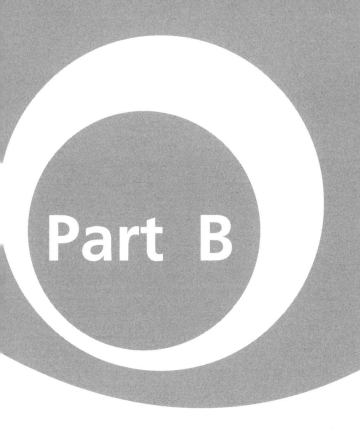

Part B

Risk and Governance

Risk: Thoughts of a Non-executive Director

Anthony J. Berry

Manchester Metropolitan University, UK

Introduction

Like many people I have served as a non-executive director of companies, some of which are registered charities. In the UK companies are subject to company law. Charities are subject to special legal provisions that are overseen by the Charities Commission.

Over the last decade, in the UK and internationally, there has been a wide and penetrating examination of the practice and regulation of corporate governance. Following some well-publicised examples (especially Enron) corporate policy and practice on risk management have become of central concern, as many of the chapters in this volume demonstrate. General procedural solutions have been offered, which take the general form of enterprise-wide risk management. It is unclear whether the practice of such procedural solutions increases or decreases the risks taken by enterprises, to economic benefit or detriment. A further element of the new world of corporate governance has been the increased expectations of non-executive directors in overseeing the work of the executive board members and having the experience and capability to draw attention to policy matters and to 'make waves' when required. This changes the role of the non-executive director from a useful sounding board, source of wisdom and good collegial contributions into a kind of supervisory role that undermines collegiality and the value coherence of boards. It also exposes the non-executive director to a wide range of duties and the risks of being judged as failing in these duties.

But risk policy and management is not so simple as the procedural approaches appear to suggest. From my experience risks that matter are not easily captured by procedures. In this chapter I will describe some aspects of risk management in four of the more than ten organisations I have served, from three sectors: Education, Research and Consultancy, Religious Bodies. Table 4.1 indicates the activities, risk issues and my roles. What follows is a set of small case studies after which I will draw out some common themes. The cases are drawn from educational, research and church organisations. Two issues in particular are evident: first the general problems of risk and its management in these cases; second, the risk exposure of the non-executive director in boards where far from boards having a unitary perspective – they were sometimes characterised by value pluralism, a pluralism which was evident in both policy decisions and sub group control of relevant information.

Table 4.1 Roles and Risks

Body	Activity	Risk Issues	My Roles
Educational			
ESE	Educational Services in Europe. Turnover. £200 k Assets £100 K	• Finding Financial support from Foundations and Governments. • Recruiting Students • Reputation	• Programme Director • Board Member
Research			
RI	Research, Education, Consultancy, Publishing. Turnover £1.5 m Assets. £2.5 m	• Winning Contracts • Staff capability • Pension provision • Reputation	• Board member and Charity Trustee • Chair of Pension Trustees
Church			
YF	Policy Research Turnover £100 k Assets £250 k	• Winning Contracts • Reputation • Financial stability	• Council Member and Charity Trustee
Diocese Board of Finance	Provision of Finance to house and pay for 250 professional staff. Turnover £10 m Assets £15 m[1]	• Rising Costs • Income stability • Governance procedures	• Board Director and Charity Trustee

[1] If the value of the Housing was included the assets figure would have been approx £100 m. Some dioceses do include this figure, others put it as a note to the accounts. There is some real legal dispute about the ownership of these properties, but the diocese has to maintain them.

Case Study 1: ESE

ESE, established by a consortium of educational bodies, provided a development programme both for their own staff and also for staff of other universities from across the globe. Its main risk was that its programme was its single product coupled with the fact that few of the universities could or would afford to pay the level of fees for the programme that would cover programme costs. Hence there was a continuing need to seek support from foundations and governments to assist individuals to be able to attend. In addition, the programme was delivered in a country for 2/3 years and then moved on to another country. This ensured its international flavour but also meant the regular need for the recreation of the capability to deliver the programme, partly resolved by ensuring substantial continuity of staffing from place to place. In my time as programme director I recruited staff from almost 20 countries from four continents and over one hundred students from about 30 countries and four continents. Over the period I made a small financial surplus. I later became a member of the Board of Directors.

In essence almost all the assets of ESE were put at risk each time the programme was moved. There was little need for formal risk management as the loss of the assets would have led to the closure of the programme and the winding up of ESE. On no occasion could we assign probabilities to events, nor did we try. Risk was managed by assuring that the appointed programme director was capable, that the host institution would provide adequate facilities as agreed at marginal costs together with the assumption that if we could find the finance there would be a good cohort of course members (reputational effect). Board members assisted the director in recruiting staff for the programme. This was not difficult as the reputation was such that many staff were happy to be associated with ESE and work for acceptable but lowish fees. The principal risk was loss of reputation. Hence the director of the programme was given resources for marketing to maintain presence and reputation, by ensuring delivery was at a high standard and that the students would be glad to recommend the programme to others. This meant that the first offering in a new country was likely to make a small loss. The other reputation management process was to refuse overtures for consortium membership from institutions that were perceived to be of a lower status and to ensure that the present group were happy to remain. There was no 'formality' to these delicate processes, but they were continually being mobilised and reinforced by board member behaviour as they participated in international academic conferences and meetings, especially those that represented institutions rather than academic bodies.

Case Study 2: RI

RI, an independent foundation, had an international reputation earned by a long series of research and policy publications and educational services. The educational work (of wide international reach) was based upon established programmes with a steady income but very small margins. It had been started up well before the great expansion of universities and of university research. So during the 50 years of its existence its work had not diminished in quality or volume but its 'market share' and hence public profile has somewhat diminished. I will touch on three issues of risk management: Contract bidding; Risk Management approaches and Pension provision.

The rise of competition for research contracts had also led to a falling bid success ratio. This was further aggravated by the size of contracts becoming smaller and the focus of contracts becoming more sharply defined. An additional factor was that public universities had little idea of costs and tended to bid for contracts at what were heavily subsidised prices, as they did not include any overhead charges. Hence more and more effort was being put into bidding for contracts (some of which the managers either knew they would not get or did not want; there was a risk of not being in the game). Further the monitoring of failed research contract bids suggested that RI quality and price were too high. The likelihood of winning was reducing; but the likelihood of winning was that the contract would be subsidised by RI. This meant that there was pressure to move from research contracts towards commercial consultancy work. This led to the recognition of a risk of losing the focus or mission of RI and becoming (however capable) a money-making body. An alternative view of this was seeking to move towards problem centred projects that could offer the space for learning. The board were divided over this strategy.

The principal risk control tools of RI managers and Board were the cash flow projection and the success and bidding rates. The cash flow projection (revised monthly) typically oscillated up and down over 15 to 20 months (issues of timing and of forecast accuracy) and then became a 'cash cliff' as no income was scheduled. So everybody was accustomed to the state where only about 1 year forward could be predicted from contracts won with further years being an assessment (with a large variance) of likely bid winning. This led to a need to sharpen up workflow measurement and project cost accounting. Of course it was important to provide some stability of employment expectations in order to attract and retain the high quality of staff that were essential to maintain RI. But the risks of future income were clear to the staff and lead to an 'anxious' organisation.

The pension arrangements at RI were based upon a defined benefits scheme. The Trustees of the Pension Fund had contracted, with the permission of the Board of RI, with a pension provider to manage the scheme and its investments. This ensured that appropriate expertise was brought to bear. After a period of rising market valuations (in which the Board of RI took a short contribution holiday), there came a period of falling markets. These market oscillations produced pre 2000 a position where the pension fund was more than sufficient to meet projected claims and post 2000 a position where it was insufficient (all this based upon government advice regarding minimum funding requirement). Further accounting rules had changed so that the pension fund surplus or deficit had to be included in the financial statements, income and balance sheets. So the accounts (based upon historic costs) now were to include the net present value of very long term liabilities.

The risk of failure to provide sufficient funds lay with the Board of RI as employer and not with the claimants. At this point the Board decided to get the advice of a pension consultant. This advice was to close the defined benefits scheme and open a money purchase scheme, passing the risk of insufficient funding from the Board as employer to the employees as future claimants. The advice was supported by an analysis that took the worst possible case on all elements to show a cumulative funding deficit about equal to the value of the pension fund at that date. Most of the Board lacked the financial insight and knowledge to challenge the, in my view, highly conservative analysis from the pension advisors. On the Advisor's assumptions claims were to grow faster than the fund could meet them given investment at the lowest rate of return available (so called risk free). But the claim to remove risk from the Board was powerful and the Board accepted the report. The board were also mindful of the impact of future pension fund surpluses and deficits on the financial statements; an impact which could, in a very worst case, imply insolvency.

However, it was clear that if the employees would agree to some tweaking of the terms of the pension fund; to reduce the annual pension uplift to current inflation figures, to increase member contributions, to extend the contribution period by several years, by adding some other flexibility, and by a more reasonable (or less conservative) view of market invest-ments, the defined benefits scheme could be continued. In this way some of the risks were passed to the employees, especially by adjusting the future rate of increases and the length of contribution periods. In essence the definition of 'defined' was rendered flexible and the 'risks' shared more equitably between the Board and the employees. The impact on the financial statements was still acute.

At no time did anybody do a formal risk analysis or try to produce any numbers or probabilities. It was managed as a discrete event with a debate about risk without that being 'evaluated' in any formal way, apart from the question of who has to bear the risks. It was also clear that future changes could be negotiated.

Case Study 3: YF

YF had been in existence for about 30 years. It sought funding for and undertook research with a view to influencing church and public pol-icy on social and economic issues, especially those impacting upon the most marginal people. Two issues regarding risk were the management of the financial endowment and the later requirement to undertake a risk analysis as part of risk management.

The Council had used the services of an investment advisor and had held an actively managed portfolio of equity and debt. However this had become less viable as the assets were needed to support the work of the foundation. The value of financial resources was deemed to be insufficient to have a market following portfolio, exposing the foundation to a higher level of risk. Following advice and discussion YF sold its portfolio and placed its financial resources into a Charity Fund that had a policy of holding a 'market following' investment strategy. The Charity Fund also charged smaller fees than the previous advisor. The later policy meant that the market risk was accepted but the Council could discharge their duty of care and be seen not to be taking speculative risks. One aspect of the debate in Council was whether the use of one Charity Fund was increasing the risk of the foundation. One member argued that a single investment was inherently more risky than the portfolio and that we might invest in more than one market following fund.

Stimulated by the published requirements of the Charity Commission the Council of YF undertook a formal risk analysis, based upon recognition of risks, an assessment of their likelihood of occurrence and the degree of impact or consequences. A simple three-point scale was used for what might be seen as an entirely subjective assessments or as the insight, knowledge and confidence that comes from experience. This produced a matrix (below) in which the identified risks were located.

Severity of consequences	Low Risk	Medium Risk	High Risk
High		Having Inadequate Financial Resources	
Medium	Governance Issues	Staff Quality Reputation Project Bidding Project Delivery	
Low		Financial Management; Premises	

Following agreement on the matrix, Council Policies on each of these areas were reviewed and in some cases small adjustments were made. It was the policy of the Council to avoid high risks. The Management Committee was charged with the task of monitoring the risks and reporting any issues to the Council, with the Council being accountable to the AGM.

The effects of this risk analysis were mostly to reassure the Council that the foundation had been prudently managed and that there were appropriate policies in place in respect of the major areas of activity. What was not foreseen was that the foundation would be the recipient of a very large bequest that almost doubled its financial resources and considerably eased its anxieties about long-term viability.

What was also missing from these procedures was the slow change in the focus of work of the foundation. The capability and interests of the professional staff drove this change in focus. As the staff tended to stay for about 5 years there was a regular opportunity to review past work programmes and set out a new one. Over the latter 10 years the foundation had become less successful in raising project finance and had funded most of the work from its own resources. Hence the question of the viability of YF was debated. The two opposing views were: use the money and when it is gone, close down, countered with a view that the foundation should be preserved and the work limited by current investment income. These were never resolved into one agreed policy. However active steps were taken to link the staff and YF to a major educational research centre both to provide a quality context for the work and to enhance the context of the staff and the reputation of YF.

The reputation of the foundation was also important in the effectiveness of its work output. This was maintained by careful staff appointments and by recruiting new Council members who were credible in the arenas where the foundation sought to work. A further lift to credibility and effectiveness of YF was given by the opportunity to take over a journal with an established publisher and market. In addition it was possible to make a joint staff appointment with one of the most important bodies in the field. This latter link was strengthened when the Chair of the YF Council became chair of a major part of the 'important' body and a former YF employee became its executive director.

So the three most important aspects of risk management in finance, viability and reputation were included in the formal risk analysis but the management of these was more to do with chance in the case of the bequest and with proactive individuals continually aware of risks and their importance in the case of reputation. The risk analysis was helpful in providing a framework and some reassurance that YF was viable and stable.

Case Study 4: The Diocesan Board of Finance (DBF)

The DBF was a registered charity and a company limited by guarantee. The membership of the Board was made up of the senior clergy of the Diocese, clergy elected from the clergy members of the Diocesan Synod and lay members elected from the lay members of the Diocesan Synod. The chair was directly elected by the Diocesan Synod. There were also several co-opted members. The primary task of the DBF was to provide finance to support the clergy (stipends, housing, pensions, national insurance, education and training). This took up about 90 per cent of the expenditure. The other 10 per cent was to support the other work of the national church, and the work of the diocese, its complex legal administration, lay ministry training, mission, social responsibility and so on. The income of the DBF came from voluntary contributions from the parishes (organised via a process of allocation of a required amount), fees paid for clergy services, interest on balances and fees for some educational services. While not an intentional policy, it was the case that the total of the allocated income shares to each parish met the total costs of the clergy. The DBF was required to produce a formal risk analysis. This task was given to a sub committee, The Finance and General Purposes Committee. They in turn gave it to the finance officer who made a very good stab at it, focusing upon work domains, risk recognition, assessment and management. However the paper, presented to the DBF for approval, was incomplete and inappropriate in some areas. While only one member commented on the paper, it was, because incomplete, noted rather than approved. There was a request that the paper be reconsidered and represented at a future meeting but this was not done. The following year a similar paper was presented for approval. Again it was incomplete. It was proposed by me and accepted by the DBF that a new sub group be formed to review the risk analysis, to take advice and to present a revised paper to the board. The DBF then appointed four of its members, including me, to the new group. However in the next 9 months, despite requests, the group was not convened and so no work was done.

The following four issues illustrated the governance risk issues of the DBF. The first of these was the handling of the management letter that the auditors send to the board. This is addressed to the members of the Board. However the letter was not given to the members. When the chair of the DBF was asked why the letter was not provided the response from the president (not the chair) was 'when we have answered the points raised you can have it'. When the papers were made available the reply had already been sent to the auditors. The following year the letter was not provided but members were told they could see a copy if they asked for it. This interesting arrogation of power was accepted by almost all of the members with those few who questioned matters being regarded as making trouble. In the next year the management letter was provided to the DBF.

The second issue was around conflict of interests regarding the financial support of the DBF for clergy. Eight members of the DBF were clergy and therefore in receipt of DBF financial support. Indeed it would be difficult to argue that they were not direct beneficiaries of the charity. There was a clear conflict of interest between the overall responsibilities of the clergy members for the collective governance of the charity and their personal interests. This matter was not resolved except that the clergy members absented themselves from direct decisions about the level of stipends. The risk here is that the overall work of the DBF would be compromised, that personal interests would shape the wider work of the DBF.

The third issue was the control of the housing maintenance budget. This was of the order of eight hundred thousand pounds per annum rising to over one million. The Budget was used to maintain and improve clergy housing. Large sums were expended during a vacancy to upgrade houses for a new incumbent. (In one case an incumbent had over 25 years refused permission for a diocesan surveyor to check the property. Nothing was done to insist on the right of access. When the incumbent retired it cost over eighty thousand pounds to repair roof and water problems.) While it was difficult to schedule work, it was also the case that the budget figure was always overspent considerably, giving rise to pressure on other budgets. It appeared that some members of the DBF were prepared to ignore the authority of the DBF to control budgets. It was as though clergy were able at will to make demands on the financial resources of the DBF. Questions at DBF meetings as to the control of the budget were met with statements that all work had to be done! The risk here was that on this issue the authority of the DBF was continually undermined by senior staff with DBF members choosing to be powerless in support of their legal authority. Here the risk was that good governance would be continually undermined with the acquiescence of most of the DBF members.

The fourth issue was the provision of financial information to the DBF. This was a continuing issue. The request by two members for formal quarterly financial and management accounts was refused on the basis that the information was of little value and that many members of the DBF would not understand it (in a number of cases this was probably true[2]). The meaning of the view that the information would be of little value was on the basis that nothing changed so the apportionments of income and expenditure would produce meaningless data. After some more pressure occasional financial reports were provided, but in 2006/07 no financial information was provided to the DBF over a 9-month period. It seems that the governance requirements of Charities and companies were not to be entertained by this DBF. It also seems that the risks of an in-group losing control or sharing governance with other members were of more significance than the risks of poor governance.

The DBF was also subject, as are many charities, to a risk of not raising the income it needed to meet its planned commitments. Over 20 years the income problem had changed dramatically. At the start of that period the Church Commissioners had been able to pay for over 70 per cent of the clergy stipends, national insurance and all of the pensions. By the end of the 20-year period the church commissioners were unable to pay any of

---

[2] It is the duty of Charity Trustees to ensure that they have the information to undertake their roles and to ensure that they understand it.

the stipends and national insurance and the DBF had to find these monies and a pension contribution of about 35 per cent of stipend. In effect this meant that an allocated share to a parish had changed very considerably. An example here was a parish that in the early period had been allocated a share of eight thousand pounds and were now allocated fourty thousand pounds. This was occurring over a period where only 20 per cent of the parishes were growing in numbers, while some 50 per cent were declining in numbers. As the allocation was based upon a 3-year rolling average of parish income it meant that the larger parishes were paying much more than the smaller, even though there was a lower contribution rate on incomes over £100 thousand (a falling marginal tax rate).

A new allocation method was proposed. This was done by the DBF being asked by representatives of the evangelicals[3] to appoint a group to examine the share allocation method. The DBF set up the group with a membership that made a recommendation. This was to change from a parish share based upon actual reported parish incomes to one based upon a standard charge, adjusted by an assessment of potential income of the population that lived in the parish boundaries. This assessment was based upon the distribution of social classes within each parish but there was no assessment of whether the contributing parishioners were a sample of the local population. Indeed across the whole diocese some 30 per cent of local parish church members did not live in the parish to which they belonged. Hence it was very unlikely that the new basis of assessment was just or even fair. However the new system relieved about fifty of the largest (by membership) and richest (by income) parishes of a contribution of about 0.5 million per annum and loaded this on to the one hundred poorest and smallest parishes, leaving about ninety parishes unchanged. This new scheme was approved by the Diocesan governing body, by a vote that represented the changes, with the unaffected supporting the change. There was a risk that the new system would lead to a reduction of income to the DBF. The risk of loss of income was quite clear but ignored. The larger parishes were on the whole evangelical in orientation and they argued that they should not be asked to support 'failing or shrinking'

---

[3] There are three broad groups in the church: Evangelicals, Liberals and Anglo Catholics. But these groupings have fuzzy boundaries. The DBF had a substantial majority of evangelicals.

parishes.[4] There were arguments that it was the Christian duty of the rich to help the poor, but that the new allocation scheme was 'punishing' the poor.

Over the next 3 years the percentage of allocated parish share contributed from the parishes fell from over 99.5 per cent to about 95 per cent with some parishes promising to try to make up the backlog. Given the limited value of DBF reserves this began to trigger changes in work and in the number of clergy.

---

[4] It was ironic that in the new system the individual church members in the larger and richer parishes would be expected to contribute about half as much as the individual members in the smaller and poorer parishes. This was excused as an example of the economies of scale.

Discussion

These four cases are not meant to be in any way representative of their sectors or a research study of risk management in the organisations. They are accounts of my experience. However I expect that other Board members in three of the cases would be in broad agreement with my observations. But you will understand that my account of matters at the DBF would be contested.

Risk management procedures

In my various roles I have attempted to contribute to the development of effective risk management. In the case of ESE there was little formal risk management but the key risks were well understood and the board set out to manage the organisation in full understanding of the risks and set out to manage them. But there was no formal documentation. In the other three cases there was a formal process. In the case of YF the introduction of a formal risk management exercise did clarify the range of risks, did lead to some minor changes and did lead to some change in accountability. But the major financial and reputational risks were handled by direct council member actions noting the delightful surprise of the bequest an event which had not entered any risk analysis. In RI there was an acute understanding of risk and how to manage them from avoidance, mitigation and management. However the largest risk, the pension fund, came to dominate discussion and cast the largest shadow.

In the DBF there was a requirement for a formal risk management process, although the paper prepared by the financial officer was not complete and the risk sub-group did not meet.

I would have to observe from my experience that the formal risk-management processes did serve to bring issues together, but it seems unlikely that very much was changed, for the worse or the better. We knew what the risks were and gathering them together made us aware of them but the management processes were in place. It was as though we could see the risks that came with the mission and which we had to manage because of the kind of organisations we were. There was never any real discussion of changing the nature of the organisation, except for the contested idea of RI becoming a consultancy organisation or of spending all of YF's money and winding it up. The formal processes may have been educative in some limited sense for some of the directors and staff. But I do not recall anybody expressing any great surprise at any of the papers. Maybe if we had understood how to hedge, but we could not quite see how to off load our risks on to another organisation. Maybe this has been done and there are, as always, things to learn.

Unitary assumptions and plural values

In the cases of RI and DBF, risk management was an openly micro political exercise, where different groups in the organisations sought to transfer risk to other members of the organisation. This was initially something of a surprise as most risk literature seeks to see organisation as unitary, but here the value pluralism became part of the material for understanding and working with risk.

It is also commonly understood that Boards would work with a unitary model especially with respect to the members of the board. This was clearly not the case in the DBF where a small central group sought to obfuscate, limit and deny information to other board members as part of an apparent strategy of maintaining a close control over the policies and finances of the organisation. The four issues of the management letter, continuation of conflicts of interest, the continuing abuse of authority regarding budgets and the denial of proper financial information to members of the board (not to mention the lack of capability of some members) demonstrate that the micro-politics were contributing to an increasing risk of governance failure and a weakening of the role of the DBF members. These issues were further marked over the new allocation of income requirements where the risk of loss of income was of less importance than relieving some groups and burdening others.

In RI the debate over pensions had some of the same qualities of internal risk transfer possibly creating higher organisational risks due to staff disaffection. The use of ultraconservative assumptions in an analysis was it seems designed to polarise issues rather than seek a solution to a real problem. It was as though risk transfer over pensions was more important than taking a wider or longer view.

This issue of unitary assumptions and value pluralism allied to micro political aims must be mirrored in many other organisations, both charitable and commercial. Given what we can learn from biography, autobiography and media accounts of intra organisational conflicts about strategy, technology, investment, promotion and dismissal it seems that the unitary assumption of formal risk management is disturbingly weak. There is a task to understand that risk management prescriptions such as EWRM or COSO. Simply add another theatre to the arenas of contestability within organisations (that this is misunderstood is exemplified by the media comment[5] about the relationship of Mr Blair and Mr Brown, where conflict and contestability is viewed as somehow wrong and a bad thing, whereas I see it as inevitable and healthy). So there is work to do on what we might see as the dialectics and contestability of risk management. Of course in conflict some will use risk management processes to lower the risk of their part of the organisation and enhance that of others, probably to the detriment of the whole organisation. But of course risk assessment, being largely judgemental and subjective, does lend itself to difference in views and hence management decisions. This same conflict reappears in the difference in risk bearing as between shareholders and managers (or the shareholders' servants). What the moral basis is for the distribution of risk between these parties is beyond my analysis here, except that it does seem perverse to claim from a unitary perspective that the shareholders' interests should be paramount.

Models and probabilities

Risk assessment in my experience was almost always judgemental and subjective and contestable. In none of these cases in risk management was there any attempt to construct probabilities or measures of risk other than simple judgements of risk as being low, medium or high. It may be that all of us were technically incompetent but it was difficult to see how such probabilities

---

[5] Media in the UK seek to polarise almost all issues into good and bad and winners and losers, and see compromise as weakness – how very curious that is!

could be calculated. There was no event or very inadequate data from which statistical analysis could be conducted. For example when the new allocation method was put to the DBF I put all the financial and other parish data into SPSS and calculated the effects on parishes, especially the redistribution of income demands from the rich to the poor. I used this analysis to demonstrate that the likelihood of the poorer parishes being unable to meet the larger allocations would increase, with a consequent loss of income (or an increase in the risk of loss of income). This was more or less ignored and nobody invited me to set out the material in a paper for consideration by the DBF. So this was of no importance to the proposers and it seemed likely that no other member of the board (or the staff) had the technical competence to understand what I had done, nor was any person interested in a proper exploration. Nor was it possible for members to understand the explanation that the adjustments based upon socio economic categories was both inadequate as a method and unjust in practice. In RI, YF or ESE there was no attempt to construct models or calculate probabilities even though in RI and ESE there was plenty of high technical competence.

The personal risk of non-executive directors

Not only did I have to consider the risks confronting these various organisations but also the risk to myself, as a director and trustee and as a professional person. While all the organisations carried indemnity insurance for directors and trustees this was only valid if we behaved with proper care within the requirements of law governing company directors and trustees. I was not sure that the insurance would be valid in the case of the DBF where some Board members were acting politically to distribute risks within the organisation, or where the necessary information for financial management was not provided to all board members or where blatant conflicts of interest were tolerated. On reflection I came to the conclusion that being a member of the DBF was professionally unsafe as all my attempts to improve matters had failed. It would come as no surprise that I decided that I would not seek re-election to the DBF.

However this issue of the increased demands made upon non-executive directors by the emergence of new requirements for corporate governance including risk management is of considerable importance, the non-executive, attending six board meetings a year, with perhaps a role in a sub committee, is expected to be able to hold the executive directors to account, this can only be done by assuring oneself that proper procedures were in place, that the audit, internal and external, reports were properly done and acted upon. But you can see that as this progresses, the non-executive role is shifting from that of a collegial board member to that of becoming a de facto supervisory board. Now that may be desirable, but it also just shifts the process up a level. The issue in here is the distinction between external regulation and self-regulation. This debate is old enough but your conclusion about it will depend upon whether you consider that trust (capability and functional) among boards is no longer possible; whether you understand that the costs and benefits of external regulation are very difficult to assess and whether you think from a functional/positivist or a social constructionist epistemology. For myself I think that the self-regulation principle is the right way to proceed but I can understand how others might differ. If the self-regulation principle is followed then the role of the non-executive can remain collegial (with some robustness in the college!); if not then I think that the role of the non-executive is almost impossible and must inevitably become supervisory. Of course this change would increase the risk of exposure of the non-executive. For here the non-executive as supervisory could be sued for negligence when any failure occurs, as all failure could be interpreted as supervisory failure, however absurd that might actually be.[6] The required returns for such risk bearing might become very high indeed.

Conclusions

In these four cases the contribution of formal risk management was valuable but limited. Risk was considered in domains and not as an organisational-wide phenomena, mainly because there appeared to be no way in which it could be so captured. Of more importance was the proactive insight of Board members. But surprises happen, sometimes very pleasant.

In the case of two of the organisations the board did not operate with a common or unitary view of risk confronting the organisation. Value pluralism produced a diverse process with internal risk transfer being managed to the detriment of the whole organisation. Perhaps future risk literature should consider the questions raised by value pluralism in Boards.

---

[6] In the sense that Ministers are supposed to be responsible for any failure in the areas of their ministry. When any such failure occurs or more likely is perceived to occur there are ritual requests that the Minister resign. For the interested, you can consider the cases of Home Secretaries. For more amusement, consider how to sue the police if crime increases. But more seriously many people try to sue auditors for corporate failure and corporate officer wrongdoing. So far the courts have proved quite robust in these matters.

The personal risk of directors and charity trustees has increased as risk management has become more required. This has put great strain on the role of the non-executive director, perhaps requiring it to become supervisory rather than collegial. However the supervisory role carries greater personal risks.

Managing Occupational Pension Scheme Risks

Chris O'Brien

Nottingham University Business School, UK

Introduction

It has been common for firms to reward their employees with pensions as part of their remuneration package, and the size of pension fund assets in the G10 countries is about $17000 billion (end-2005), with five of the ten counties having pension fund assets exceeding 50 per cent of gross domestic product (Swiss Re, 2007).

Pensions are, however, a long-term obligation that cannot be costed precisely, meaning that pension provision involves a significant risk that the cost differs from what firms have expected. This risk has become more apparent as new accounting standards, particularly IAS19, have required a more rigorous assessment of, and disclosure of, pension scheme assets and liabilities. At the same time, we have seen pension liabilities increasing as a result of low interest rates and an increase in the expectation of life, while schemes that were invested in equities in the bear market of 2000–2003 suffered a major shock to their assets.

These risks have been reflected in many schemes having a substantial deficit, the top 50 firms in the eurozone had assets only 70 per cent of the liabilities at the end of 2006 (Mercer HR Consulting, 2007).

The risks arising from occupational pension schemes are therefore important but, for most firms, the risks do not relate to the core skills of the firm. This chapter therefore seeks to identify the pension risks that firms face, and how they can be managed.

We study defined benefit (DB) schemes, where the rules of the scheme define the pension benefits payable to members. It has been common for the pension to be defined as a specified fraction (e.g. 1/60th or 1/100th) of the employee's final salary, that is. the salary in the year before he or she retires, multiplied by the number of years he or she has worked for the employer. A member of a scheme with a pension fraction of 1/60th, who works for 40 years, would therefore be entitled to a pension of two-thirds of his or her final salary. While employees may, and typically do, contribute to the scheme, it is the employer who bears the residual risk that the cost of providing the benefits is different from what was expected.

This is in contrast to defined contribution (DC) schemes, where the rules specify that the benefits for a member are what can be provided from the contributions paid (by employer and employee). Therefore the cost is set (e.g. 10 per cent of salaries) and it is the employees who bear the risk that the pensions are different from what they expected. DC schemes are also called 'money purchase' schemes. The liabilities of such schemes should be no more than the value of the scheme's assets, so they should never be in deficit.

In order to identify the risks to which firms are exposed, we need to understand how the financial position of defined benefit pension schemes is assessed. The risks are in three categories, the first of which is 'liability risks', being the uncertainty about the benefits that will be payable. 'Asset risks', concerning the scheme's investments, and operational risks are the other two categories of risk. These matters are all discussed within this chapter together with an illustration of how firms may respond to risks by discontinuing or changing the nature of the scheme itself.

The financial position and risks of defined benefit pension schemes

Measuring the financial position of pension schemes

Employers bear the risk that defined benefit pension schemes turn out to be more costly than they envisaged. It is therefore important to consider what affects the cost of providing pensions, and how the finances of the scheme appear on the firm's balance sheet. This leads on to identifying the risks to which the firm is exposed.

Pensions accounting has been the subject of much debate in recent years, and the International Accounting Standards Board's standard, IAS19 (last revised in 2004) requires firms to show the assets and liabilities of their DB pension schemes on their balance sheet. A deficit within the scheme therefore leads to a reduction in the net assets of the firm.

The assets of the scheme are at market value under IAS19. The calculation of liabilities is, however, more complex: firms calculate the discounted value of pension entitlements that have accrued to date. For example, in a scheme where the pension fraction is 1/60th, for an employee who has worked for the firm for 10 years, and is due to receive his or her pension in 15 years' time at age 65, the liability is calculated as the present value of the instalments of pension expected to be paid:

- the pension amount equals 10/60ths of the employee's estimated salary at retirement; such estimated salary equalling current salary increased by an assumed rate of salary increases over the next 15 years;
- starting in 15 years' time, and payable until the death of the pensioner, (and, if applicable, increasing in accordance with the scheme rules);
- taking into account the probability of the employee leaving service or retiring other than at normal retirement age, with a consequent amendment to the amount of benefit payable;
- allowing, where relevant, for the employee choosing to commute some or all of his or her pension for a cash sum;
- adding in the payments that may be paid to the pensioner's widow or widower; and
- discounting all payments back to the balance sheet date at the rate of interest on high grade corporate bonds.

This calculation needs several assumptions, in particular regarding:

- salary increases (and price inflation, if this affects the amount of benefit);
- mortality rates;
- employee withdrawal and early retirement rates;
- the proportion of pension benefits commuted for cash, and the terms on which this commutation takes place;
- the proportion of members married at date of death (and age of widow or widower); and
- the discount rate to be used.

It is the actuaries' role to assess the cost of pension schemes, choosing appropriate assumptions as part of this process and advising firms accordingly. However, actuaries may have provided an estimate of this cost without necessarily highlighting the range of possible outcomes (Morris, 2004). Assumptions are only assumptions; reality will be different. We expect firms to be especially concerned about downside risk and, in particular, the increase in liabilities that can arise from high salary increases or an increase in the expectation of life; and the risk that the investment return on their assets is less than what they were assuming.

Not all schemes use the IAS19 basis for their calculations. In Switzerland, a discount rate of 4 per cent per annum is commonly used to value the liabilities, whereas long-term government bonds are yielding only 2 per cent. Publica, the scheme for Swiss civil servants, reported assets at 108 per cent of liabilities at the end of 2005, but acknowledged that moving to a true bond-based method would change this to 84 per cent (Evans-Pritchard, 2007). However, although such accounting methods may conceal the risks, the risks are still present and, if not transparent in the accounts, may fail to be addressed.

One other concern is that IAS19 itself may not fully reflect the firm's exposure. If a firm wished to transfer its liabilities to a third party, such as a life insurer, the amount it needs to pay is essentially a 'fair value'. However, there is evidence from the UK that this exceeds the liability typically recorded in the firm's accounts. Firms therefore ought to be concerned that, should they wish to transfer these risks, this imposes a cost above what they have provided for.

Identifying the risks

We can now identify the risks that pension schemes expose firms to (Figure 5.1).

Some of the risks to the employer are 'liability risks', relating to the amount of benefits payable, the form in which they are payable, and the duration for which they are paid.

The amount of pension depends, in particular, on the rate of salary increases. The nature of this dependence is a consequence of the scheme rules; for example, as an alternative to basing pensions on a member's final salary, pensions may be related to members' average revalued salaries, where each year's salary is revalued up to retirement, perhaps in proportion to changes in prices. If that is the case, price inflation affects the benefits payable, and the difficulty of

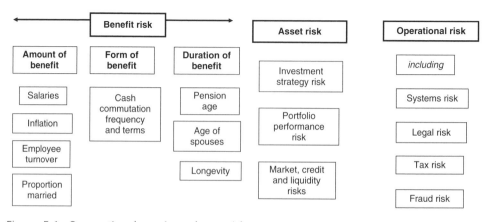

Figure 5.1 Occupational pension scheme risks

forecasting it brings further risk. Price inflation may impact on the amount of benefit payable in other ways as well: for example, pensions in course of payment and deferred pensions may be increased in proportion to price changes.

If an employee leaves service before pension age, his or her benefit reflects this, and changes in employee withdrawal rates are therefore relevant to the cost of the pension scheme and the uncertainty of the cost.

The rules may also grant pensions to widows or widowers, which therefore leads to risks since the firm will not know the proportion of pensioners who are married at the time of their death.

The form of the benefit can also affect the costs of the scheme. Members may be able to commute some or all of their pension for a cash lump sum. Depending on the cash commutation factor (i.e. what cash is granted in lieu of £1 per annum pension) commutation may provide either a loss or (more likely) a gain to the pension scheme. The cost of the scheme will therefore depend on members' choices to commute or not.

The duration over which pensions are payable depends on the age at which pensions begin to be paid and on how long pensioners live. While the pension age is normally the age at which employees retire from the firm, it is not necessarily fixed and, indeed, some flexibility in pension age can be a valuable way of managing these risks. However, if there are exogenous changes in pension age, perhaps arising from legislation or reflecting social trends, that is a source of risk.

Longevity risk is the risk that employees live for a longer (or shorter) time than expected, thereby changing the value of the benefits payable. A related point is that firms may not know the ages of members' spouses; if they turn out to be younger than anticipated, the cost of widows' and widowers' pensions will exceed what was expected.

In addition to liability risks, firms are also exposed to asset risks. If the firm valued its liabilities by discounting at a high grade corporate bond yield, it could invest the scheme assets in such bonds to protect itself from the effect of changing interest rates. In practice this is not so easy, and the price- and salary-linked nature of the liabilities causes further difficulties. In any event, schemes may invest in a range of assets, including equities: these may give the prospect of higher returns but introduce new risks.

There are also operational risks, which we consider later in the chapter.

Incentives to manage risk

Before we consider pension risks in more detail, we need to ask, do firms need to be concerned by these risks? After all, firms have shareholders with diversified portfolios, who may not want firms to forgo profits in order to reduce risks. However, there are a number of valid responses to this, in particular the following:

- Some firms, including small family firms, may not have diversified share-holders, and the shareholders may wish to manage risks to avoid the risks to their individual wealth.
- The asset risk may affect the firm's beta.
- There are a number of reasons for firms with diversified shareholders to manage risks: for example to reduce the cost of financial distress if the pension risks lead to the firm experiencing large losses.
- These are not core risks for most firms, and it would arguably be better if these risks were borne by other parties with greater relevant expertise or capacity for bearing these particular risks.

We therefore go on to consider how pension risks can be evaluated and managed.

Liability risk

Amount of benefit

The risks regarding the amount of benefit payable concern the following:

- Salary growth, impacting on salary-related benefits.
- Price inflation, where pension increases depend on price inflation.
- Withdrawal rates (members leaving service early), and
- The proportion of members where benefits are payable to widows or widowers

Salary growth is an area where firms can make assumptions, but these may not be robust. Say we consider an employee aged 25; we are looking to estimate his or her salary at retirement in 40 years' time. Cardinale et al. (2006) calculated the ratio of real wages in the UK in 1890 compared to 1850, 1891 compared to 1851, and so on, up to 2001. This ratio averages 1.66 but 5 per cent and 95 per cent percentiles are 1.13 and 2.15. We conclude that, for an employee aged 25, estimating salary at retirement in 40 years' time, is subject to considerable uncertainty.

Salary growth risk has a general dimension and a specific dimension. If salaries in general rise faster than expected, the cost of a pension scheme is naturally higher than otherwise. The firm's salary experience may also differ from general trends. This problem may be exacerbated, particularly in small schemes, if large salary increases are awarded just before retirement, especially if these awards are to already high-paid employees.

There is an argument that salary risk is not a true risk to the firm since it controls what salary it pays. However, in practice, it can be difficult for a firm to determine the salary for an individual in a way that takes into account the implications for pension cost. Is it feasible to restrict the salary increase for an employee approaching retirement on the grounds that a large increase for him or her leads to a high cost to the pension scheme in a way that it would not for a younger employee? If an employer has both defined benefit and defined contribution schemes, is it feasible to have different salary structures? This is logical, but raises practical problems.

Salary risk may be addressed in other ways. One is to say that the firm will be protected if it invested in assets, the price of which was linked to salary levels. Such investments do not exist, though. Now, it can be argued that if a pension scheme invests in equities, this would be a reasonable match, because the price of equities tends to rise faster when the economy is doing well and hence salaries are rising. However, as we shall see, the equities-salaries link is quite weak, and does not justify pension schemes having a substantial investment in equities.

Firms may mitigate the salary risk by specifying that salary rises above a certain level are to be ignored in determining pensionable salary.

Alternatively, the salary risk can be mitigated by changing the form of benefit from being based on the employees' final salary to average revalued salary. Revaluation may be in accordance with price inflation but, if so, this brings an exposure to price inflation risk. That risk can be mitigated by a number of possible actions, although the firm's choice may be constrained by legislation such as:

- placing an upper limit on the revaluation in any one year;
- by making increases discretionary; or
- increases being made subject to the finances of the scheme permitting it.

Rates of price inflation may also affect pension scheme costs if pensions in course of payment and/or deferred pensions are linked to price levels. It may be possible to manage this risk by investing in assets that are linked to price changes. However, the risk can also be controlled in other ways. One possibility is for the increase in pensions to be at the lower of price inflation and some pre-determined rate, such as 5 per cent ('limited price indexation'). In the Netherlands, firms' commitments to pensions are usually not inflation-linked, but they decide, in each year, whether to increase pensions, depending on the scheme's financial position (Swinkels, 2004). Giving the firm discretion over the amount of benefit is a flexibility that can be valuable in managing risks, but will reduce the attractiveness of pension schemes to the members.

The importance of the withdrawal rate risk depends on the value of the benefits on withdrawal. Traditionally, the benefits to employees on withdrawal were relatively low, resulting in the pension scheme gaining; however, this may be regarded as unfair to such employees, and pressure (or regulatory requirements) to increase benefits for early leavers may have neutralised this gain.

A greater risk may be the employees retiring early on generous terms, which leave the pension scheme worse off. Early retirement may be offered at the employer's discretion, and this risk can therefore be controlled by not exercising this discretion unless it is neutral from the perspective of the scheme's finances or for specific reasons such as it being part of a redundancy programme that is justified on a cost–benefit basis. Where discretion is exercised by the trustees, this is more difficult.

Another area of uncertainty is the marital status of members. It is common for schemes to provide a pension to the widow or widower of a member. However, many firms do not know whether or not scheme members are married. Firms may assume that 90 per cent of members are married, adding about 12 per cent to the cost of the scheme. If firms obtained information on marital status, they can reduce the uncertainty regarding what the actual proportion is. Alternatively, if the firm provides data on the postcode (or address) of members, then linking this to a database of individuals can provide reasonably accurate information on marital status. Certainly, for a scheme looking for an insurance company to buy out the scheme benefits, this kind of information can be valuable in enabling the cost of the buy-out to be assessed more precisely and, with the insurer requiring a lower loading for uncertainty, at potentially lower cost (Richards, 2006).

Quantifying risks

Having identified these risks, how can they be quantified? One approach is to use stress tests, involving assessing the impact on the scheme's finances if alternative assumptions regarding salary growth, price inflation, and so on applied. For example, we may assume salary growth is at some higher level permanently or we may assume it follows some deterministic trend. The tests may involve more than one variable changing, but the alternative assumptions should still be mutually compatible. Stress tests do not tell us the probability of the assumptions tested actually arising, but they help identify what are the risks which, if they materialised, would have financial implications sufficiently large to cause concern to the firm.

A more sophisticated approach is stochastic modelling, used by many actuaries in advising firms with pension schemes. This involves designing an economic scenario generator, which produces some hundreds (or thousands) of possible future scenarios, each involving a series of interest rates, price inflation and salary growth in the years ahead. The firm can then calculate the probability of various economic outcomes, although some caution is necessary: the precise figures produced by models reflect the assumptions in the construction of the model, and different models will produce different answers. These models are run in conjunction with the pension scheme assets, so we return to this subject later in the chapter.

Stochastic modelling can be used to produce summary measures of risk. One commonly used indicator is Value at Risk (VaR), which is 'X' in 'I am 99 per cent (for example) confident that the financial position of the pension scheme will not worsen by more than £X'. Hawkins and Moloney (2006) indicated that most pension scheme risks can be quantified using Value at Risk (VaR), with the main risk typically relating to real interest rates.

Form of benefit

We saw previously that the cash commutation option may lead to schemes making a loss or gain. The risk can be controlled by having a policy of ensuring that commutation factors (they will differ by age and sex) change as interest rates and the expectation of life change, so as to ensure that commutation is financially neutral for the scheme. However, there may be legislative or practical constraints on this; and, indeed, ensuring financial neutrality may not be an appropriate objective.

However, if neutrality is not an objective, the risks have to be recognised. Some firms have increased commutation factors in response to an increasing expectation of life, having previously taken credit for gains assumed to arise upon employees commuting on factors that were consistent with the expectation of life as applied in the past. Good risk management would have identified the potential for the increased costs that have resulted.

Duration of benefit

Assessing the value of the liabilities of the pension scheme requires assumptions about how long the pensioners will live. This valuation uses mortality rates in actuarial tables, but such tables are only an estimate of the rates that will apply in the future to the scheme's pensioners, and uncertainty about pensioner lifetime is a significant risk.

This risk can be considered in two parts. First, what is the current set of mortality rates applicable to the scheme membership; and, secondly, how might such rates change in the future?

A firm can reduce the uncertainty about its longevity exposure if it has a good understanding of the expected longevity of its pension scheme members. A large firm will have data on the mortality rates of pension scheme members in past years, and this can be used as the basis for making adjustments to standard mortality tables. For most firms, though, the data is not sufficiently robust to make this feasible. However, we know that mortality rates depend not only on age and sex but also on occupation, social class and geographical area. Firms may therefore be able to assess, broadly, that the expected mortality experience will differ from that of the population as a whole. Firms employ actuaries to carry out the valuation of their liabilities, and it is right to question the actuaries to understand what mortality assumptions they are using, and why.

However, techniques have been established whereby a firm can understand the likely mortality experience of scheme members more precisely. If the firm has information on the postcodes (and, preferably, precise addresses) of the pension scheme members, it may be possible to link such information to a database with information on the socio-economic status (and possibly other characteristics) of individuals. Since we know there is a link between socio-economic status and mortality, we can thereby estimate the mortality experience of those individuals. The uncertainty regarding future mortality rates can therefore be narrowed down.

Richards (2006) demonstrates how such an analysis was applied to a portfolio of life insurance company pensions. Nineteen per cent of them fell into mortality group 1, where the expectation of life for a 65-year-old male was 23.1 years; 5.4 per cent in group 4 (21.4 years), 2.5 per cent in group 7 (20.6 years) and so on. It was possible to categorise 78.7 per cent of pensioners into such groups, increasing the confidence in estimating longevity.

The further element of uncertainty is how will mortality rates change in the future? The rapid, but also unpredictable increase in expectation of life can be illustrated by trends in the UK. The expectation of life of a 65-year-old male in 2004 was estimated in 1981 as 14.8 years, whereas in 2004 it was estimated at 19.0 (Pensions Commission, 2004). Improvements in medical treatments and a decline in smoking are among the factors that have contributed to this trend. Also connected with this surge in the expectation of life is the 'cohort effect', where individuals born in 1925–1945 have experienced significantly greater reductions in mortality rates compared to their predecessors, while the succeeding generation has had mortality improvements that have been rather lower (Willets, 2004). However, the causes of this cohort effect are not well understood, and actuaries have used alternative assumptions on how strongly the cohort effect is expected to continue.

The mortality risk may be illustrated by stress tests. For example, the impact of an extra year of life can be estimated, generally adding 3–4 per cent to pension liabilities. This gives no indication as to how likely such a change is. One way of addressing this is to build a stochastic model of mortality, using it to project mortality rates in the future with confidence intervals. An example of this is in Dowd et al. (2007). The problem, however, is that such models are developed on the basis of past data, and we do not know how different the future will be. For example, a cure for cancer, an increase in obesity or an influenza pandemic will upset the calculations. Uncertainty necessarily remains.

What techniques are open to firms to mitigate this longevity risk? They may be able to transfer some of the risk to scheme members; to insure their liabilities with a life insurance company; or may wish to purchase a financial instrument from the capital markets in order to hedge the risk.

The risk may be transferred to scheme members by raising the scheme's pension age, such that the expected duration of pension payments is unchanged. Firms may be able to effect such a change only for future accruals, although it is open to them to negotiate some change in the entitlement to accrued benefits if they wish to apply the new pension age to all pension benefits.

Raising the pension age may be just one means of responding to a pension scheme deficit. However, a firm could link longevity risk to pension age more formally, as done in the BAe Scheme, which has had a substantial deficit. As the expectation of life rises, employees will be given the choice of working longer or accepting a reduced pension. This deal was struck after bargaining which also involved the firm paying additional one-off contributions to the scheme as well as increasing the annual contribution rates both for the firm and its employees.

Buying an insurance policy is a more usual way of managing longevity risk. Insurers have traditionally offered annuities: a firm can pay a single premium to the insurer, which takes responsibility for paying the pensions in course of payment. Annuities not only transfer longevity risk, but also pass the investment risk to the insurer, which gives the insurer the potential to make investment profits. The fact that insurers are regulated should mean that the risk of default is very low. Insurers may also buy out deferred pensions, but they clearly cannot take over the salary-related liabilities of current employees. In any event, longevity risk is much greater for scheme members who are currently in service, where what is relevant is the set of mortality rates some 50 years or more ahead, which is a risk where life insurers are less enthusiastic.

The final option is, possibly, for firms to transfer the risk to the capital markets. The resources of the capital markets are significantly greater than the capital of insurance companies, so is there the potential for a financial instrument, the payments from which depend on mortality rates in such a way that the payments are higher if expectation of life increased. Such a longevity bond was proposed by Blake and Burrows (2002), but it was not until 2005 that such a bond was offered on the markets. It was to be issued by the European Investment Bank, involving BNP Paribas and Partner Re, but it did not attract support and was withdrawn. It may be that the specific product design was unattractive (Blake et al., 2006) and that the lessons learned will enable a different financial instrument to be launched successfully in the future. The launch in 2007 by JP Morgan of an index of mortality rates and expectations of life may help a market develop. However, firms will be conscious that financial instruments based on some mortality index will not necessarily follow the mortality trends of the firm's employees, so there is a significant basis risk. At this stage, firms appear unenthusiastic about hedging the risk in the capital markets.

Asset risk

Investments pose a major risk for pension schemes. The main debates in this area are: whether bonds or equities are more suitable for pension schemes; and whether firms should adopt liability-driven investment (LDI). We focus on choice of investment strategy although, in practice, firms also need to consider the risk that the actual investments chosen perform differently from that expected, given the strategy.

Firms' ability to manage the asset risk may be constrained by the responsibilities that trustees have for investment. Different stakeholders (shareholders, bondholders, employees, government, consultants) have different interests in investment strategy (Chapman et al., 2001), although firms will clearly wish to have a say in what is decided.

The cult of equity for pension funds was promoted by George Ross Gooby, who invested the whole of the Imperial Tobacco pension fund in equities. One argument for investing in equities is that, in the past, equities have produced returns significantly higher than those on bonds, the equity risk premium being about, say, 4 per cent. It is argued that these higher returns reduce the costs to employers, and with a long time horizon, there is time diversification, with years of good and bad returns averaging out, so that risks are reduced.

A rather different argument is that equities are a good way to control risk because they match pension scheme liabilities. Firms need to invest in assets which increase as salaries increase; although equity returns and salaries may move in opposite directions in the short run, they are expected to move together in the long run. If the shares of capital of labour in national income remain constant, then equities and salaries are expected to increase at the same long-run rate, therefore equities provide a good hedge for salaries over the long run.

However, there are contrary arguments. Certainly, pensions in course of payment and deferred pensions are bond-like liabilities where the logical starting point is that bonds are the matching assets, with inflation-linked bonds playing a part if pensions are inflation-related. The matching argument can therefore potentially only apply to salary-related liabilities.

Smith (1998) analysed what was the risk-minimising portfolio for UK national average earnings over 1922–1997: he found that gilts and index-linked gilts are of prime importance, with equities having only a small role. Exley, Mehta and Smith (1997) found that index-linked bonds are a much better match, compared with equities, for salaries. Van Bezooyen and Mehta (1998) also found that the minimum risk portfolio for pension schemes in the Netherlands was largely fixed-interest securities as opposed to equities, especially for pensioners but also for active members. Cardinale's (2004) study found a link between equities and salaries, concluding that equities and property would feature in a minimum risk portfolio for salary-related liabilities. Some other analyses over a number of countries have found negative correlations between earnings and equity returns, the results not providing any support for the view that equities are a good hedge for salary risk (Sutcliffe, 2005). This approach has been accepted by a number of schemes, notably Boots, which moved out of equities into bonds (Ralfe, 2002).

In practice, matching using bonds poses problems. Pension scheme liabilities are long-dated, and bonds of sufficiently long duration may be unavailable, leading to re-investment risk (Cardinale et al., 2006). In addition, suitable inflation-linked bonds may not exist. Where firms accept that bonds are a suitable hedge, the bonds can be subject to credit risk. There is also liquidity risk, although pension obligations in the short-term are relatively predictable, so this should not be a major issue.

Cardinale et al. (2006) suggest that the existence in pension schemes of unhedgeable risks may mean it is appropriate to have a higher allocation to equities than otherwise. Another argument is that as perfect hedges are not feasible, a diversified portfolio of imperfectly matched assets may reduce risk (Booth et al., 2004).

Many pension schemes have persisted with a high equity exposure, although there are significant differences internationally. The proportion of assets in equities (in 2005) was over 40 per cent in the UK, Ireland, Netherlands and Belgium, under 20 per cent in Germany and Portugal (Moloney, 2006). The 2005/06 accounts of National Grid show that its UK scheme had 41 per cent in equities, whereas its US scheme had 66 per cent.

The debate about pension scheme assets is not merely about bonds or equities: it has moved on to the meaning and merits of liability-driven investment (LDI). This uses the cash and risk profile of the liabilities to derive the assets that are an effective hedge. In practice, the liabilities can be complex; for example, if pensions are subject to Limited Price Indexation.

Kemp (2005) suggests that a simple LDI portfolio could be structured using an underlying physical component, typically an actively managed bond portfolio, based on the nature of the liabilities; and a swaps overlay component, consisting of swaps or other derivatives to better match the liabilities. The rich diversity of swap markets is used because the long duration of liabilities means physical bonds cannot match adequately. Many firms prefer to retain asset risks rather than adopt LDI, however, perhaps because LDI requires buying bonds and derivatives that lock in what are perceived to be low returns. Some wish to retain some risky assets that are expected to produce a high return, which may be, for example, hedge funds, real estate or private equity.

Given the different theoretical views and practices about investment strategy, firms must understand and measure the investment risks they are running. The marked sensitivity of the deficit in UK pension schemes in the event of alternative interest rates or equity levels was illustrated by the Pension Protection Fund and The Pensions Regulator (2006). The more sophisticated approach of stochastic modelling has been increasingly applied in order to produce future projections of the financial position of schemes. A model can be used to answer questions such as what is the likelihood of the assets being less than the liabilities over some future period. The model can then be re-run using alternative investment strategies and/or alternative employer contribution rates in order to assist decision-taking.

Speed et al. (2003) illustrated how pension schemes could measure risks using a 'Liability Benchmark Portfolio' (LBP), being the assets that would maintain the current relationship between assets and liabilities as economic conditions change. They envisage the LBP comprising bonds of various types. They go on to describe how a stochastic model can be run, producing a pattern of the value of assets and liabilities over time in each of the scenarios being generated. This can be done using alternative investment strategies, to illustrate confidence levels for the performance of the assets compared to the LBP, and the probability of underperformance compared to the LBP.

As investment risks have become more apparent, interest in LDI has grown. The Dutch arm of British American Tobacco assesses its risks using VaR, finding that 55 per cent of its risk related to interest rate and inflation exposure, 45 per cent to investment returns. It announced a move to an LDI strategy, with half of the interest rate and inflation rate risk to be hedged using swap overlays (Woolner, 2007). However, many firms appear cautious about some new forms of investment strategy: UK pension schemes have been reluctant to use derivatives to hedge interest rate and inflation risk (Association of Corporate Treasurers and Mercer HR Consulting, 2006).

Operational risks

Firms are also subject to operational risks in their occupational pension schemes. There are operational risks about the assets, as was illustrated when Robert Maxwell defrauded the Mirror pension schemes in the UK. Inadequate systems are also a source of operational risk.

However, a risk that is especially difficult to control is legal risk: pension schemes have been subject to increasing regulation in recent years, which can lead to higher expenses in the running of the schemes, together with the risk that regulations will require firms to pay a higher level of benefits than originally contracted for; for example, by ensuring that employees who leave service receive not less than some minimum specified pension. Somewhat different is the risk that firms are making in their pension schemes may be open to legal challenge.

Changes in tax rules are another source of risk. When the UK decided in 1997 that pension schemes would no longer be entitled to reclaim tax credits on dividends, the overall cost of pension schemes to UK employers increased by around £5 billion per annum.

Overall scheme responses

Some firms have responded to the increased cost and new perceptions of risks in defined benefit pension schemes by looking to curtail their pension obligations, thereby cutting both costs and risks.

Many employers have therefore closed their DB schemes to new entrants. New employees are enrolled in a defined contribution scheme, where the employer does not bear inflation, salary or longevity risks. Some firms have gone further, by ceasing future accruals under defined benefit schemes for existing members. Those employees will in future participate in a DC scheme, so that their pension at retirement would be made up of pensions arising from the two schemes.

Another step is for firms to eliminate risks by legally transferring their liabilities to a third party. This is feasible provided there are no salary-related benefits continuing to accrue. In the UK an increasing number of life insurers are prepared to buy out scheme liabilities in this way. A number of new insurers specialising in this area (e.g. Paternoster) pay particular attention to the risks involved.

Somewhat different from a scheme buyout, a pension scheme may offer to buy out the pension rights of individual members. This could be particularly attractive to members who left service with deferred pensions (who may be able to consolidate the pensions they have from different sources) and to firms, if the transfer value is less than the IAS19 liability. However, while some UK schemes have been progressing this approach, it is open to criticism that it may not be in the members' best interests.

Firms may wish to manage risk by sharing risks with scheme members. They may do this by:

- having discretion over what benefits are payable, particularly what may be thought of as non-core benefits, such as increases in payment or early retirement benefits (although, in some schemes, this discretion is held by the trustees);
- using their discretion regarding the contributions payable by employees, although an increase in contributions may require negotiations;
- formally linking changes in benefits and/or employees' contributions to the scheme's financial position, or to the occurrence of specific circumstances that adversely affect the scheme; for example, high real salary increases or an increase in the expectation of life.

One possibility is that firms offer employees the option to continue their current rate of contributions but with a lower future accrual rate, or to increase their contributions to maintain accrual rates. However, it is not clear to what extent employers would be able to continue to share the risk with employees in this way. For example, should a deficit arise as a result of a decline in stock prices, employees may respond by saying that the adverse outcome of a risky investment decision should not impact on employee contributions.

Firms may seek to renegotiate accrued benefit in order to share more of the risks with scheme members. The Association of British Insurers (2007) commented, 'This would require robust mechanisms to identify the willingness of staff to accept cuts in benefit, and allocate the renegotiated surplus fairly'.

The contrast in risk-bearing between DB and DC schemes is stark, and perhaps there is some scheme design that incorporates some elements of both DB and DC sharing risks between employer and employees (Lewin and Sweeney, 2007).

A solution that involves stakeholders sharing risks more explicitly is advocated by Ponds and Quix (2003). They describe the way in which most Dutch pension funds struggled with underfunding following the fall in stock prices, with stakeholders disagreeing on how to recover solvency. They say, 'The implicit nature of the contract may be harmful to the continuity to the contract. However, the current situation can be regarded as a challenge to reach a more explicit contract of risk-sharing. Such an explicit pension deal will prevent policy inertia and conflicts between stakeholders, because it is always clear who has to pay, when, to what extent, in a shortage situation'.

If risk-sharing is to be more formal, this demands more formal risk management. Puttonen and Torstila (2003) found deficiencies in risk management of Finnish pension funds, and only a small number carried stress testing on their portfolios. Recently, more thought has been given to pensions risk management, with better risk quantification, and greater consideration of risk control. The Chartered Institute of Management Accountants (2006) and Hawkins and Moloney (2006) are examples of an increasingly methodical approach to risk management in pensions.

Concluding comments

New accounting rules for DB pension schemes have increased the profile of pension costs and risks. Increasing longevity and adverse financial conditions have forced firms to review how they operate their pension schemes, many of which have been in deficit.

That deficit has been recognised by scheme trustees as, essentially, an unsecured creditor of the scheme. It cannot be taken as granted that the firm will make up a deficit, and Gordon et al. (2005) consider the 'sponsor covenant'. This corporate credit risk for trustees can be mitigated in a number of ways (Hawkins and Speed, 2005). For example, they could:

- strengthen the obligations of the firm, such as gaining an agreement that no prior debt will be created or a clause whereby a deficit in the scheme becomes immediately payable if the firm is taken over;
- obtain third-party support by a letter of credit or though credit insurance; or
- buy relevant market instruments, such as a credit default swap, which provides a sum in the event of insolvency or a default of debt.

It is clear that the firm and scheme members have different interests, and they will have different approaches to risk. Employees do, however, bear some of the DB scheme risks, as has been apparent from increases in employees' contributions when the scheme has run into trouble. It is the unclear nature of the sharing of risks that has caused concern, and alternative (but more formally agreed) ways of sharing risk in the future may have advantages. We bear in mind that many employees have been automatically forced to accept investment and longevity risks when their employers discontinued their DB and established a DC scheme. So if the continuation of a DB scheme requires some agreed participation of members in the risks, it is not necessarily unacceptable.

The appearance of deficits has led firms to look to cut their pension costs in order to eliminate the deficit. However, this is an inadequate response. Firms need to examine the risks that the pension scheme exposes them to, and manage those risks. That does not necessarily mean eliminating those risks. It means assessing what are the risks that firms can sensibly bear. There should then be appropriate controls to manage risks and report ongoing risk exposures. Pension schemes may differ in nature from firms' core processes, but this is an important reason why pension risks must be incorporated in firms' risk management processes.

References

Association of British Insurers (2007). 'Understanding companies' pension deficits' ABI research paper 3.

Association of Corporate Treasurers and Mercer HR Consulting (2006). 'Survey of pension financial risk'. http://www.treasurers.org/technical/resources/tt_mercer_risksurvey.pdf.

Booth, P., Chadburn, R., Haberman, S. James, D., Khorasanee, Z., Plumb, R.H. and Rickayzen, B. (2004). *Modern Actuarial Theory and Practice*. Boca Raton: Chapman & Hall/CRC.

Blake, D. and Burrows, W. (2002). 'Survivor bonds: helping to hedge mortality risk', *Journal of Risk and Insurance*, Vol. 68, No. 2, pp. 338–348.

Blake, D., Cairns, A.J.G. and Dowd, K. (2006). 'Living with Mortality: Longevity Bonds and Other Mortality-Linked Securities', *British Actuarial Journal*, Vol. 12, No. 1, pp. 153–197.

Cardinale, M. (2004). 'The long-run relationship between pension liabilities and asset prices: a cointegration approach.' Paper presented to the Staple Inn Actuarial Society.

Cardinale, M., Katz, G., Kumar, J. and Orszag, J.M. (2006). 'Background Risk and Pensions', *British Actuarial Journal*, Vol. 12, No. 1, pp. 79–134.

Chapman, R.J., Gordon, T.J. and Speed, C.A. (2001). 'Pensions, Funding and Risk', *British Actuarial Journal*, Vol. 7, No. 4, pp. 605–662.

Chartered Institute of Management Accountants (2006). The pension liability: managing the corporate risk.

Dowd, K., Cairns, A. and Blake, D. (2007). Facing Up to the Uncertainty of Life: The Longevity Fan Charts, Paper presented to the 29th UK Insurance Economists' Conference, Nottingham University Business School.

Evans-Pritchard, B. (2007). 'Deferred judgement', *Life & Pensions*, April, pp. 8–12.

Exley, C.J., Mehta, S.J.B. and Smith, A.D. (1997). 'The Financial Theory of Defined Benefit Pension Schemes', *British Actuarial Journal*, Vol. 3, No. 4, pp. 835–938.

Gordon, T., Evans, A., Freeman, G., Forrester, N., Hall, R., McKay, N. and Shellswell, S. (2005). 'Allowing for the sponsor covenant in actuarial advice', Final Report of the Sponsor Covenant Working Party of the Actuarial Profession London: Institute of Actuaries.

Hawkins, J.W. and Moloney, M. (2006). 'Measure it to manage it', *The Treasurer*, November, pp. 24–27.

Hawkins, J. and Speed, C. (2005). 'Forging the pension trustee', *The Treasurer*, November, pp. 18–21.

Kemp, M.H.D. (2005). 'Risk Management in a Fair Valuation World', *British Actuarial Journal*, Vol. 11, No. 4, pp. 595–712.

Lewin, C. and Sweeney, E. (2007). 'Deregulatory Review of Private Pensions: A Consultative Paper.' http://www.dwp.gov.uk/pensionsreform/pdfs/consultation_paper.pdf.

Mercer HR Consulting (2007). 'Pension Scheme deficits and trends.' http://www.mercerhr.com/summary.jhtml/dynamic/idContent/1146050.

Moloney, M. (2006). 'An optimal structure', *The Treasurer*, September, pp. 30–32.

Morris, D. (2004). *Morris Review of the Actuarial Profession: Interim Assessment.* London: HM Treasury.

Pensions Commission (2004). 'Pensions: Challenges and Choices', *The first report of the Pensions Commission.* London: The Stationery Office.

Pension Protection Fund and the Pensions Regulator (2006). 'The purple book. DB pensions universe risk profile'.

Ponds, E.H.M. and Quix, F. (2003). 'Integral risk management by pension funds in a fair value framework', *Pensions*, Vol. 8, No. 3, pp. 222–234.

Puttonen, V. and Torstila, S. (2003). 'Risk management in Finnish pension funds: A survey', *Finnish Journal of Business Economics*, Vol. 52, No. 1, pp. 31–46.

Ralfe, J. (2002) 'Why move to bonds?' *The Actuary*, March, pp. 28–29.

Richards, S. (2006). 'Understanding pensioner longevity', http://www.richardsconsulting.co.uk/modelling.pdf.

Smith, A.D. (1998). 'Salary related cash flows: market based valuation.' Institute for Mathematics and its Applications and Institute and Faculty of Actuaries conference on actuarial valuations, accounting standards and financial economics.

Speed, C., Bowie, D., Exley, J., Jones, M., Mounce, R., Ralston, N., Spiers, T. and Williams, H. (2003). Note on the relationship between pension assets and liabilities, paper presented to the Staple Inn Actuarial Society.

Swinkels, L. (2004). 'The Impact of New Capital Requirements on Asset Allocation for Dutch Pension Funds', *Pensions*, Vol. 10, No. 1, pp. 75–81.

Swiss Re (2007). 'Annuities: A Private Solution to Longevity Risk', *Sigma*, March.

Sutcliffe, C. (2005). 'The Cult of the Equity for Pension Funds: Should It Get the Boot?', *Journal of Pension Economics & Finance*, Vol. 4, No. 1, pp. 57–85.

Van Bezooyen, J. and Mehta, S. (1998). 'Investment strategies for Dutch and UK pension funds', Working Paper, Group for Economic and Market Value Based Studies.

Willets, R.C. (2004) 'The Cohort Effect: Insights and Explanations', *British Actuarial Journal*, Vol. 10, No. 4, pp. 833–877.

Woolner, A. (2007). 'A Motivating factor', *Life & Pensions*, March, pp. 12–16.

Monitoring of the Risk Management System and the Role of Internal and External Audit

Margaret Woods* and Christopher Humphrey[†]

*Nottingham University Business School, UK
[†]Manchester Business School, UK

Introduction

Risk management is a process which has quite a wide capacity for variation in terms of organizational scale, commitment and structures. At one extreme, risk management can be a function that is comprised of a single risk champion or a part-time risk manager, whilst at the other end of the scale there may be a large and dedicated risk management department, headed up by a Chief Risk Officer.

Although levels of sophistication evidently vary across organizations (Dowd et al., 2007), an increasingly propounded view is that risk is something for which everyone in an organization carries a certain degree of responsibility in terms of its management and control. For instance, the board of directors is said to establish the risk appetite and hold ultimate responsibility for the effectiveness of risk management and internal controls. Other managers take ownership and responsibility for managing risks within their areas of work, and in so doing, directly support the board of directors by promoting compliance with the control systems and helping to engender a culture of risk awareness. Front-line workers and service staff embody a respect for this culture and work within its parameters to ensure that the organization is not exposed to undue or unplanned levels of risk. It is this type of emphasis on risk and its management that led authors such as Power to conclude that we are now living through an era dominated by a desire to risk manage everything (see Power, 2004). Other authors (see Young, 2001) have also highlighted the capacity for risk to be used as a metaphor that covers many different aspects and elements of a company's organizational system and approach to management.

Support for the effective operation of the risk management system is typically provided by a number of different parties both internal and external to the organization. Internal support is provided by the risk officer, financial director and internal audit function. Externally, such parties as customers, suppliers, business partners, external auditors, regulators and financial analysts may also provide information that aids the effectiveness of the risk management process. While these external parties complement the effectiveness of the organization's risk management process, they are clearly not responsible for the running of any such system – the effectiveness of which will depend on the ability of the organization's risk 'officers' to ensure that the system is sufficiently sensitive to capture significant shifts in risk exposure from whatever available source.

Standard risk management models portray it as a process that has a series of core elements which are used to ensure that all material risks impacting (or

Figure 6.1 Core elements of the risk management process (*Source* 'A Risk Management Standard', IRM, AIRMIC and ALARM (2002))

with the potential to impact) upon the achievement of corporate objectives are identified, prioritized, reported and monitored. Figure 6.1, which is drawn from a UK Risk Management Standard, illustrates the interdependence between these core elements, and, significantly for the purposes of this chapter, indicates the commonly assumed importance of the audit function within corporate risk management systems.

The central pillar of Figure 6.1 denotes the way in which risk management is defined or viewed in ways that link it closely to organizational objectives – risk assessment, evaluation, reporting and treatment are all undertaken by reference back to organizational objectives. The modification procedure on the left-hand side depicts a feedback process to indicate that lessons learned in the operation of the risk management system are used to review and possibly modify supporting control processes, risk management procedures and, even, organizational objectives, in order to ensure an acceptable and appropriate level of risk exposure on the part of the organization.

The established lines of responsibility and control for risk provide the core of the risk management system – and these, in turn, require ongoing evaluation if their effectiveness is to be ensured/maintained. The right-hand side of Figure 6.1 indicates that the primary responsibility for this evaluation is achieved via formal audit. The auditors are usually both internal and external to the organization, and the information collected via the audit process is supposed to be used to inform and improve the risk management system. Such frameworks present auditing as an important function that both complements and supports risk management processes and procedures. As risk management continues to climb the agenda of company executives, as well as national and international regulators, the potential significance of auditing clearly increases. However, even acknowledging the contributions of a small number of researchers working in this area, it is fair to conclude that we still know relatively little as to the respective operational role and capacities of internal and external audits in the processes of risk management. Indeed, in an era when risks are supposed to be actively managed and controlled, there is a certain irony that contemporary risk management processes appear to place considerable faith in auditing – a function that has had a problematic historical track record in terms of its capacity to meet expectations and deliver suitable levels of service quality (for reviews, see Humphrey, 1997; Humphrey et al., 1992; 2003; Power, 1996; 1997; 2003).

We currently know very little about the operational role that auditing plays in processes of risk management and the evidence/analysis that does exist is not that assuring in terms of what is being achieved in audit-oriented risk-management approaches (Griffiths, 2005). For instance, it is evident that despite a long association between audit processes and risk (see Pickett, 2005), the study of the practical impact of risk on audit plans and procedures and the extent to which audit training is being revised to take account of new risk man-agement techniques and methodologies is very much in its infancy.[1] Indeed, there are evident indications that what is possible in the audit arena, especially in terms of the external audit, is always going to be subject to a range of (polit-ical and economic) pressures associated with the institutional audit field – with a broad constellation of factors (some quite divorced from the technical capacities and capabilities of audit-testing instruments) influencing or shaping what is deemed to be legitimate (and thereby effective) audit practice.

At a more basic level, arguably, there still remains a fair degree of uncertainty over the relative roles of internal and external auditors – particularly in terms

---

[1] For an initial range of papers just published on this subject, see *Accounting, Organizations and Society* (AOS), Vol. 32 No. 4/5, July 2007.

of whether the internal audit function has been displaced, redrafted and/or reinvigorated as a result of the creation of a new risk management 'profession'? What is the role of internal audit relative to external audit and can auditors be expected to have the requisite expertise to make formal assessments of the quality of risk management systems and associated control processes?

A number of the above issues go beyond the scope of this chapter but they are important in terms of at least framing the context and intent associated with the analysis presented here. In short, this chapter has been written with the intent to facilitate and enhance understanding of the changing role and reliance on audit within the broader risk management arena – and to highlight key questions that need to be asked of such processes and associated operational assumptions/expectations. We begin by considering the role of internal audit, as this function increasingly appears to be portrayed as a central component within risk management systems.

The role of internal audit

The Institute of Internal Auditors (2007) defines internal audit as:

> an independent, objective assurance and consulting activity designed to add value and improve an organisation's operations. It helps an organisation accomplish its objectives by bringing a systematic, disciplined approach to evaluate and improve the effectiveness of risk management, control and governance processes.

According to this definition, it does not matter whether internal audit is undertaken by in-house staff, or alternatively is outsourced to a professional firm – whatever its contextual position, its role is to offer independent and objective assurance and advice. Such independence is usually sought to be secured structurally by positioning the Head of Internal Audit in a position independent of the Chief Financial Officer (CFO) – most notably, ensuring that the head of Internal Audit reports directly to the Audit Committee and not through the CFO. This reporting system is designed to try and ensure that the Audit Committee will be alerted to any problems of internal control or inadequate risk management systems, and also be in a position to oversee the effectiveness of responses to such control inadequacies. Internal audit also provides advice to managers on how to improve their risk management controls (Anderson, 2006; Pickett, 2006). Advice may also take the less structured form of management training in risk management skills, with the aim of increasing risk awareness and embedding risk controls into the day-to-day management procedures.

Beyond such general, broad-based definitional components and objectives, the precise operational role and boundaries of responsibility of internal audit can be expected to differ between organizations (see, for example, Selim and McNamee, 1999). The following list includes some of the tasks that have been found to fall within the contemporary scope of internal audit.

- Audit of risk management processes across the full breadth of an organization
- Supporting and training staff in the area of risk identification, assessment and monitoring
- Drafting of a risk-based audit plan, which focuses on the key risks identified by senior management
- Drafting and co-ordination of the risk management reports submitted to both the Audit Committee and the Board of Directors
- Providing a commentary on the effectiveness of actions taken by management to address control weaknesses identified by internal audit
- Communicating good practice in risk management
- Providing a statement of assurance on risk and internal control for the Audit Committee and the Board of Directors.

Recent changes in the role of internal audit

In considering the role of internal audit, it is important to recognize that its broader role is only a relatively recent development. For many years, internal audit was a narrower, compliance-oriented function, described by some as an 'organizational policeman and watchdog' (Morgan, 1979) – a definition not dissimilar from the external audit function, but with the latter traditionally being seen as having the greater capacity in terms of the ability to report in an independent fashion. The 1990s and beyond have witnessed a transformation in, at least, the officially claimed scope and spirit of internal audit activity – shifting it towards a more strategic assurance and advisory function (Carcello, 2005).

In the UK, for example, it has been claimed that reports such as that by the Turnbull committee on corporate governance (FRC, 2005) gave internal audit the opportunity to redefine itself as a new profession seeking to 'add' corporate value (see Page and Spira, 2004). Turnbull introduced the requirement for management to include in their annual report a statement that they had undertaken an annual review of internal controls. There was no requirement to report on the effectiveness of the controls, but merely to report that a review had been undertaken, but the need for annual review created potential scope for a rise in the status of the internal audit function. In order to prepare a corporate-wide report on internal controls for the Board of Directors, however, the internal audit function had to shift away from a purely financial emphasis. James Duckworth, the Chief Auditor at Unilever, describes the company's internal audit department as having a very wide remit: 'we are talking about overall governance as well as corporate risk management' (CIMA/IFAC, 2002, p. 39). The CIMA/IFAC report argues that 'Leading edge' internal audit departments are no longer concerned solely with the financial controls and the need for assurance that the contents of the financial statements are materially correct. Instead, their role is becoming much broader and involves undertaking work necessary to gain objective assurance on the reliability and integrity of *both* the financial and non-financial information that is used by management to monitor performance. This is achieved by an evaluation of the effectiveness of many different types of internal control, both quantitative and qualitative in nature. The growing breadth of coverage by internal audit serves to tie its role in quite closely with that of risk management. In the same CIMA/IFAC report, Sarah Blackburn, former head of global audit and assurance at Exel, argues that internal audit has become 'a central part of the art of risk management' (CIMA/IFAC, 2002, p. 43). It is now regularly claimed that recent years have seen a sea change in the role and status of the internal audit function, with the perception shifting from a view that internal audit was a dull but worthy process into one in which its role in providing independent assurance is very helpful to management and particularly to non-executive directors (Griffiths, 2005).

It is reasonable for such claims to be treated with a fair degree of caution as they often tend to emanate from internal audit departments themselves – and it is very evident that claims to jurisdictional expertise in this area are inevitably tinged with self-interested, political motives. However, it is generally accepted that, at least in the largest and most influential internal audit departments, audit methodologies applied by internal auditors have shifted towards a more risk-based approach to audit planning. Traditionally, systems would have been reviewed on a rotation basis, but risk-based internal auditing is intended to be less programmed, focusing efforts on the systems and processes that have been identified as being most at risk. For example, in a global organization it may be felt that newly established overseas subsidiaries are more likely to experience control failures than well-established units.

A risk-based approach would result in the new subsidiaries being audited more frequently.

One of the consequences of this overall shift in audit emphasis and methodological approach is a need for internal auditors to gain expertise not just in financial controls but in what are frequently labelled as 'softer' organizational controls. Whatever the nature of the risk – be it the corporate reputation, supply chain, disaster recovery, regulatory compliance or any other issue – internal auditors increasingly need the access, skills and expertise to evaluate control effectiveness and make recommendations in cases where problems may arise. The right of access to all areas of an organization is therefore fundamental but it is also important to remember that in terms of the overall effectiveness of any audit-based function, the control loop is closed only when audit findings are reported upon and the reports are used to drive improvements in the future control process. Internal audit reporting which produces information that is useful to management requires the establishment of effective lines of communication between the Board of Directors, the Audit Committee and the internal audit department/unit. Dialogue between the three parties enables internal auditors to understand more clearly the levels of assurance that are being sought, and the risk appetite and resources that define the boundaries of their work.

There are certainly a fair degree of claims pointing to the rise of internal audit in an era which has seen a growing corporate and regulatory emphasis on processes of risk management, governance and internal controls. However, it is important to note that there is also quite strong evidence of significant variations in the level of involvement of internal audit in processes of risk management (Dowd et al., 2007). Page and Spira (2004), for example, categorize the range of involvement as going from the 'outside observer' to the 'influential insider' (Page and Spira, 2004, p. 92), although this terminology is left undefined and is not reinforced by empirical examples.

Such findings match the personal observations of one of the authors in interviews with senior management from a number of FTSE 100 companies. These identified some companies as retaining a separate internal audit function, while others combined it with risk management or absorbed it within a specialist risk management function headed up by a Chief Risk Officer. Whether Page and Spira's (2004) view that internal audit will become increasingly more important is only something that can be judged with hindsight and it is still very much early days in terms of drawing conclusions regarding sustained levels of impact and operational significance. However, it cannot be disputed that internal audit is a function regularly linked with notions of risk management and that their respective future organizational significance are likely to be inherently interwined.

External audit

Discussion of the role of the external, rather than internal, auditor in relation to risk management and internal control is made complex by variations in external audit specifications contained in national regulations and governance codes.

The financial scandals of the last decade instigated the widespread introduction of governance reforms which placed responsibility for internal controls firmly in the hands of the Board of Directors. The Combined Code in the UK (FRC, 2005), the King Report in South Africa (IOD, 2002) and the Canadian 'CoCO' Guidance on corporate control (CICA, 1995) all see risk management as part of the internal control process for which the Board of Directors is responsible. Similarly, in the USA the Sarbanes–Oxley Act (SOX) of 2002 requires that companies establish and maintain an adequate internal control structure for financial reporting. Thus, in terms of where the ultimate responsibility for internal control lies, it does appear, internationally, to reside with the senior management or Board of Directors.

In order to provide reassurance to potential investors and the capital markets, it may, however, be necessary for the Board of Directors to publish some form of statement on internal control. Such a statement may take the form of a simple declaration that a review of controls has taken place, or it may also include a judgement or commentary on the effectiveness of those controls. It is at this point that there emerges international disagreement over forms of regulation and the role of the external audit.

Typically, governance regulations specify a need for management to undertake an annual review of internal controls but do not impose any requirement to report on the findings of that review. In France, for example, the Financial Security Act (loi de sécurité financiere – LSF) of August 2003 introduced new requirements on disclosures to shareholders and the market for the purposes of corporate governance and internal control, but in common with regulations elsewhere within the EU, the Act does not require publication of an external audit opinion on internal control efficiency. Across the EU, the revised 8th Directive on Company Law aims to achieve 'high-level — though not

full — harmonisation of statutory audit requirements' (EU 2006, para
a result, it is possible for a member state requiring statutory audit to im
more stringent requirements.

In Germany (and the USA), regulations have been introduced which are vari-
ants of the EU approach and both involve external auditors in the judgement
process. In Germany, the statutory regulations for listed companies require
external auditors to undertake an audit of the internal control systems and
report the results in a separate part of the internal audit report (§321 para.
4 HGB) which is submitted to the supervisory board. The external auditor is
required to mention any improvements that are necessary in relation to the
risk management system, and whilst specific suggestions are not required in
the audit report, they can be included in the management letter. Most importantly, however, the external auditors' report is for internal and not external
circulation.

This regulation is limiting insofar as it confines the exposure of the external
auditor's judgement to within the firm. Interestingly, although such a regulation does not exist in the UK, past experience suggests that such commentaries
would form a natural part of the management letter submitted by external auditors. In other words, the German regulation could be regarded as a codification
of existing (best) audit practice.

In contrast, Section 404 of SOX in the USA goes further by imposing a requirement for a public company to include within its filing an assessment by the
management and their external auditors as to whether the company has an
effective system of internal control over its financial reporting. The Securities
and Exchange Commission (SEC) filing is in the public domain and hence the
assessment is public.

The USA thus stands alone in imposing upon external auditors a responsibility for externally reporting their evaluation of internal control effectiveness
although the assessment only relates to controls over the financial reporting
process. This regulatory position has caused protestation within the audit profession, as well as provoking extensive complaints about the high costs of
compliance, although there has to be competing recognition of the increased
audit fees generated through post-Enron regulatory initiatives (Sneller and
Langendijk, 2007).

Implicit in the rules laid down under SOX is a belief that reliability of financial reporting can be achieved via a combination of tight internal controls
and external independent audit. The direct link between audit and reliability

...uestion because of the difficulties associated with both
...ol effectiveness and also constructing a framework for
...spirit of SOX section 404 is not open to dispute, there
...nies and audit firms are experiencing problems in rela-
...tion (see Gupta, 2006). As reported in Chapter 2, Alan
...chairman of the US Federal Reserve Bank, has predicted
that there will be changes made to the rules governing mandatory internal
control certifications.[2]

Two linked sets of guidance have been issued for use by companies and auditors in the implementation of Section 404. The first is Auditing Standard No.2
(AS2), issued by the Public Company Accounting Oversight Board (PCAOB).
This Auditing Standard requires both management and external auditors to
conduct their internal control assessments by reference to an internal control framework that is deemed acceptable by the SEC. Both AS2 and the SEC
final rules state that the COSO 1992 Framework entitled 'Internal Control –
Integrated Framework' (COSO, 1992) constitutes an acceptable assessment
framework – resulting in COSO 1992 being used by virtually all US companies.
For non–US-based companies, the SEC also accepts both the Turnbull guidance and CoCO as alternative acceptable evaluation frameworks, presumably
on the grounds of a similarity of overall approach.

Even using these guidelines, the problems in implementing Section 404's
requirements on assessment of control effectiveness have led to a rethink by
the SEC. In their 2006 report, the SEC reiterated the view that the evaluation
methodology cannot be prescribed because circumstances will vary from company to company. Much more fundamentally, they revised their view of the
COSO 1992 Framework in this regard. The SEC (SEC, 2006, p. 6) state that:

> While the COSO framework identifies the components and objectives of an effec-
> tive system of internal control, it does not set forth an approach for management
> to follow in evaluating the effectiveness of a company's Internal Controls over
> Financial Reporting (ICFR). We, therefore, distinguish between the COSO frame-
> work as a definition of what constitutes an effective system of internal control
> and guidance on how to evaluate ICFR for purposes of our rules.

This change of view significantly downgrades the importance of the COSO
1992 Framework as a point of reference for US public companies. The reasons for the change in the guidance are multiple, but Gupta (2006) suggests
that one key factor may have been that companies and auditors were focusing

---

[2] See page 44–45 for further commentary.

on a bottom-up approach to assessment rather than the top-down and more cost-effective way that was originally envisaged by the legislation. He concluded that the bottom-up approach results in a failure to focus on the real risks facing the business.

A similar emphasis on clarity and rigour was evident in the Public Company Accounting Oversight Board (PCAOB, 2005) report on the Sarbanes–Oxley requirement for an external audit report on internal controls relating to financial reporting. The report criticized auditors for taking too uniform an approach to internal control testing and for not adopting a more thoughtful, risk-based approach, a view also supported by the SEC. Subsequently, in May 2006, the PCAOB announced a four-point plan to improve auditors' implementation of the internal control reporting provisions (PCAOB 2006). Nevertheless, subsequent regulatory reports from the PCAOB (2007) have remained critical of the ongoing lack of application by some audit firms of a risk-based approach in assessing company internal controls.

The standard risk control system defined earlier (see Figure 6.1) identified important roles for the audit function. Internal audit monitors the effectiveness of internal controls and provides independent guidance and advice on how they might be improved. External audit provides additional assurance through further testing of internal controls and monitoring of internal audit. The key question suggested by the above, albeit limited, review of internal control assessment under acts such as Sarbanes–Oxley is what role should be realistically expected of audit and the relative contribution of internal and external audit?

Company directors have a fiduciary duty to protect the assets of the shareholders and use their funds efficiently and effectively, and breaches of that duty can lead to fines and imprisonment. Directors are answerable because they are responsible for the day-to-day running of the organization and have a duty to keep themselves informed about control problems that may threaten the achievement of objectives. External auditors are reliant upon information provided by staff internal to the organization, and whilst they have legal rights of access to that information, they do not exercise daily control over decision making, and can be expected to limit their capacity/responsibility for assessing the effectiveness of internal control systems and risk management more generally. Arguably, it could be said that SOX is asking auditors to accept liability for a judgement that is made with excellent *but not complete* knowledge. It could also be claimed that a SOX-oriented reliance on external audit is encouraging businesses not to take an enterprise-wide exposure to risk and is engendering a culture of micromanagement of low-level controls that deal only with the reliability of financial reporting. Such claims and questions raise a broad, fundamental issue in terms of the efficacy of risk management systems that rely heavily on (external) audit processes. In short, how auditable are such systems and the risk-related data being produced by such systems?

The challenges associated with formulating an external audit opinion on internal control efficiency have been widely debated within Europe as the EU attempts to reach a conclusion about its own regulatory response to Sarbanes–Oxley. The Federation des Experts Comptables Europeens (FEE) invited comment on its discussion paper 'Risk management and internal control in the EU', which was published in March 2005, and the responses from accounting regulators, professional accounting bodies and professional audit firms were firmly against the introduction of SOX-type legislation within the EU. For example, the Institute of Chartered Accountants of Scotland declared that:

> we believe that any regulations/guidance should cover all internal controls and should not be limited to financial reporting controls. We would oppose any movement towards a rules based approach such as the US Sarbanes-Oxley Act and believe that it would not be appropriate for boards to make a statement on the effectiveness of the company's internal control or for there to be any expansion of the external auditors' responsibilities on this matter. We believe that it is impossible to make such a statement in real time and any statement as to effectiveness relating to a past period risks giving misleading signals about its continuing relevance (ICAS, 2006, p. 2).

The views expressed reflect a general recognition of the persistent uncertainty about the feasibility of asking external auditors to comment on internal controls. The letter submitted by PricewaterhouseCoopers included the observation that:

> Auditors *can* provide assurance on internal controls, but this will depend on the nature of the subject matter to be evaluated, the auditor's experience, and whether there is a framework of established criteria by which to make an evaluation (PWC, 2006, p. 5).

In other words, the practitioners view is that the precise role of the auditor in such a process remains open to debate and further discussion is needed before regulatory requirements can be imposed. In contrast, one academic (Holm, 2007) suggests that external auditors ought to recognize that they must be perceived as the experts regarding internal control and risk management and that this must be engrained as part of the service rendered, that is, part of the value-adding nature of an audit. The debate therefore continues.

The auditability of risk management systems is an issue that goes beyond the auditor's capacity to respond to SOX-based requirements. To consider such an issue one has to adopt a perspective that sees auditing as something rather more complex than a simple technical process involving the examination of rational and verifiable data. Indeed, the role of audit in processes of risk management is increasingly requiring auditors to make supposedly 'objective' assessments of evidently 'subjective' estimates. For instance, financial data such as asset valuations in a balance sheet are increasingly likely to have been prepared on a fair value basis. Likewise, the valuation of the liabilities of a defined benefit pension fund in terms of the present value of expected future cash flows is highly subjective. The size of such cash flows is dependent upon a range of assumptions, including the life expectancy of the fund members, but mortality figures are open to question. Actuaries construct life expectancy tables on the basis of current knowledge, but that knowledge is continually evolving and open to more than one interpretation.

External auditors may use their own actuarial experts to verify both the underlying assumptions and the resulting fund valuations, but the process only gives 'reasonable assurance' and not certainty that the figures are accurate. In other words, the widely regarded perception that verifiability and auditability are synonymous concepts is open to question (Power, 1996). While it can be argued that external auditors have always had to work with uncertainty and been required to make subjective estimates in forming their audit opinion, the growing number of areas in which such subjective judgement is required can only mean that the profession is going to be open to potentially greater criticism that it is not working in a fashion that accords with client or public expectations.

This clearly resonates with the notion of an auditing expectation gap but the issues are more profound than those traditionally encountered historically on this topic. This is because it is not clear exactly on what expertise base external auditors have to make assessments on processes of internal control and risk management. It is also not clear to external users precisely what auditors have or have not done in arriving at their audit opinion.

These isues are well illustrated by considering the growing use of highly specialized risk-modelling techniques for the valuation of risk exposures. One such model which is growing in popularity is 'Value at Risk' or VaR. VaR is defined as the maximum potential loss a portfolio may incur due to adverse movements in market prices, given a certain holding period and confidence interval. For example, a daily VaR of £5 million with a confidence level of

98 per cent implies a risk of a loss of that sum twice in every hundred days if current positions are left unchanged for a full day. It is an estimate only.

Can auditors expect to be given access to the raw data that is used to compile the VaR numbers, or simply the resulting statistics? In what proportion is the responsibility for confirming the VaR figures published in the annual report being divided between internal auditors and external auditors? Does the inclusion of a VaR figure in the annual report imply that the external auditors believe that it represents a true and fair view of the institution's risk exposure? The answers to these questions are unclear under current regulations, including Audit Practice Note 23 (APB, 2002). However, the questions are significant because VaR information is virtually impossible for outsiders to audit or otherwise verify. Even the most advanced VaR users have great difficulty with model validation or backtesting. A reasonably large number of backtests are available, but the ability of these tests to distinguish between 'good' and 'bad' models can be dubious, mainly because of the relatively small amounts of data available on which to carry out backtests. Clearly, if the institutions themselves have difficulty validating their own models, any external auditor, who inevitably knows a lot less about the institution and its risk models, will have real problems.

More fundamentally, the data required for model validation/verification are quite different from traditional accounting data. For example, accounting profit and loss (P/L) data is typically calculated according to standard principles of accounting prudence, which often means that assets are valued at amortized cost and fluctuations in their values are smoothed over. However, for risk-measurement purposes it is more important to use data that reflects underlying volatility rather than accounting prudence. Hence, the P/L series needed for model validation will usually be very different from a P/L series based on traditional accounting principles. Consequently, external auditors need to have sufficient knowledge to request the appropriate form of data for model verification, and recognize the way in which this can be reconciled with the data included in the published accounts.

A related problem is the fact that professional training for auditors is centred around financial accounting practice and regulation, and does not include detailed statistical study at the level necessary to review and verify VaR procedures and results. To require audit of risk information would therefore involve considerable revision of the content of accounting education and examinations. It would therefore seem that the audit of VaR information poses big potential problems for the auditing profession, and these issues are currently the matter of ongoing debate between the big audit firms and accounting standard setters.

The growing complexity of financial instrument trading and the financial engineering practices that surround such activity suggests that VaR is probably not the only area where the auditability of the data may be brought into question. If so, then it is important that the profession ask regulators to consider whether or not they are being asked to perform an impossible task. For the moment, it seems reasonable to conclude that the role of external audit in the risk management process is far from clear-cut. There is also certainly considerable scope for exploring the contribution of audit to processes of risk management. Covaleski and Dirsmith (2003) highlighted the political nature of battles between different professional bodies to establish global legitimacy/expertise in the field of assurance services. A similar, ongoing positioning can be seen by respective interested parties in relation to SOX-based initiatives and it remains an ever-pressing issue to know about what is being done or achieved by external audit in the name of risk management. It may well be that internal audit is in a potentially stronger position in terms of being able to access the benefits of the current commitment to risk management but there is an overriding requirement regarding the need for more empirical information on the work of internal and external auditors.

Conclusion

This chapter began with a brief outline of a risk management framework which appeared to define a role for formal audit, and continued with an analysis of that role in respect of both internal and external audit. There is little that is contentious about the role of internal audit, as it serves to independently monitor and advise on internal control processes – although there is empirical evidence to suggest widespread variations in the precise nature and style of the interface between internal audit and risk management. The position of external audit, however, looks far less secure and there are residing questions as to the potential overlap between the work of internal and external audit and the efficacy of risk management systems that place such a significant emphasis on external verification (FEE, 2006; Power, 2005; Holm, 2007; Allen, 2006). There remains a very significant empirical research question in the sense of a real need to know more about what is being done in the name of audit and what is being 'added' by external audit investigation and reporting. Likewise, should external users of corporate annual reports be demanding that companies provide more detailed reports on risk exposures rather than rely on independent but poorly specified audit reports and associated assurance provision?

References

Allen, R.D. (2006). 'Auditor Risk Assessment: Insights from the Academic Literature', *Accounting Horizons*, Vol. 20, No. 2, pp. 157–177.

Anderson, R.J. (2006). 'Unearth the Power of Knowledge', *Internal Auditor*, Vol. 63, No. 5, pp. 58–64.

APB (2002). *Audit of Derivative Financial Instruments, Practice Note 23*, Auditing Practices Board, London.

Carcello, J.V. (2005). 'Changes in Internal Auditing During the Time of the Major US Accounting Scandals', *International Journal of Auditing*, Vol. 9, No. 2, pp. 117–127.

CICA (1995). *Guidance on Control*, Canadian Institute of Chartered Accountants, Toronto.

CIMA/IFAC (2002). 'Managing Risk to Enhance Stakeholder Value', IFAC, New York.

Committee of Sponsoring Organisations of the Treadway Commission (COSO) (1992). *Internal Control-Integrated Framework*, AICPA, New York, NY.

Dowd, K., Bartlett, D.L., Chaplin, M., Kelliher, P. and O'Brien, C. (2007). 'Risk Management in the UK Insurance Industry: The Changing State of Practice', *International Journal of Financial Services Management*, Special Issue (forthcoming).

EU (2006). Directive 2006/43/EC of the European Parliament and of the Council of 17 May 2006 on statutory audits of annual accounts and consolidated accounts, amending Council Directives 78/660/EEC and 83/349/EEC and repealing Council Directive 84/253/EEC.

FEE (2006). 'Analysis of Responses to FEE Discussion Paper on Risk Management and Internal Control in the EU'. Brussels. Available electronically on http://www.fee.be/fileupload/upload/Risk%20Management%20and%20Internal%20Control%20in%20the%20EU%20Discussion%20Paper%2005031282005121024.pdf.

Financial Reporting Council (2005). *Internal Control – Revised Guidance for Directors on the Combined Code*, London.

Griffiths, P. (2005). *Risk Based Auditing*. Gower, Aldershot.

Gupta, P., (2006). *COSO 1992 Control Framework and Management Reporting on Internal Control: Survey and Analysis of Implementation Practices*. IMA, Montvale, NJ.

Humphrey, C. (1997). Debating Audit Expectations, in M. Sherer and W.S. Turley (eds), *Current Issues in Auditing*, 3rd edn, Paul Chapman Publishing, London, pp. 3–30.

Humphrey, C., Moizer, P. and Turley, C.S. (1992). 'The Audit Expectations Gap in Britain: An Empirical Investigation', *Accounting and Business Research*, Vol. 23, No. 91A, pp. 395–411.

Holm, C. (2007). 'Risk and Control Developments in Corporate Governance Changing the Role of the External Auditor?', *Corporate Governance*, Vol. 15, No. 2, pp. 322–333.

The Institute of Chartered Accountants of Scotland (ICAS) (2006). Downloaded from the FEE site on http://www.fee.be/fileupload/upload/Scotland2742006471452.pdf.

Institute of Directors (IOD) (2002). *The King Report on Corporate Governance for South Africa 2002*. Institute of Directors in Southern Africa, Parktown, S.A.

Institute of Risk Management (IRM), The Association of Insurance and Risk Managers (AIRMIC) and ALARM, (2002). *A Risk Management Standard*. London.

Institute of Internal Auditors (2007). 'What is Internal Audit?' Published on http://www.iia.org.uk/about/internalaudit/.

Morgan, G. (1979). 'Internal Audit Role Conflict: A Pluralist View', *Managerial Finance*, Vol. 5, No. 2, pp. 160–170.

Page, M. and Spira. L. (2004). *The Turnbull Report, Internal Control and Risk Management: The Developing Role of Internal Audit*. Institute of Chartered Accountants of Scotland, Edinburgh, Scotland.

Public Company Accounting Oversight Board (PCAOB) (2005). Report on the Initial Implementation of Auditing Standard No. 2, An Audit of Internal Control over Financial Reporting Performed in Conjunction with an Audit of Financial Statements, PCAOB Release No. 2005-023, Public Company Audit Oversight Board, Washington.

Public Company Accounting Oversight Board (PCAOB) (2006). 'Board Announces Four-Point Plan to Improve Implementation of Internal Control Reporting Requirements'. Published on http://www.pcaobus.org/News_and_Events/News/2006/05-17.aspx.

Public Company Accounting Oversight Board (PCAOB) (2007). Report on the Second-Year Implementation of Auditing Standard No. 2, An Audit of Internal Control over Financial Reporting Performed in Conjunction with an Audit of Financial Statements. PCAOB Release No. 2007-004, Public Company Audit Oversight Board, Washington.

Pickett, K.H.S. (2005). *Auditing the Risk Management Process*. Wiley, Hoboken, N.J.

Pickett, K.H.S. (2006). *Audit Planning a Risk Based Approach*. Wiley, Hoboken, N.J.

Power, M. (1996). 'Making Things Auditable', *Accounting, Organizations and Society*, Vol. 21, No. 2/3, pp. 289–315.

Power, M. (1997). *The Audit Society: Rituals of Verification*. Oxford University Press, Oxford.

Power, M. (2003). 'Evaluating the Audit Explosion', *Law & Policy*, Vol. 25, No. 3, pp. 185–202.

Power, M. (2004). *The Risk Management of Everything: Rethinking the Politics of Uncertainty*. Demos, London.

Power, M. (2005). 'Organizations and Auditability: A Theory'. Paper presented at the Centre for Theoretical Studies in the Humanities and Social Sciences.

PricewaterhouseCoopers (PwC) (2006). Downloaded from the FEE site on http://www.fee.be/fileupload/upload/PwC2742006551448.pdf.

Securities and Exchange Commission (SEC) (2006). *Management's Report on Internal Control over Financial Reporting*. File number S7-24-06.

Selim, G., and McNamee, D. (1999). 'The Risk Management and Internal Auditing Relationship: Developing and Validating a Model', *International Journal of Auditing*, Vol. 3, pp. 159–174.

Sneller, L. and Langendijk, K.H. (2007). 'Sarbanes Oxley Section 404 Costs of Compliance: A Case Study', *Corporate Governance*, Vol. 15, No. 2, pp. 102–111.

Young, J. (2001). 'Risk(ing) Metaphors', *Critical Perspectives on Accounting*, Vol. 12, pp. 607–625.

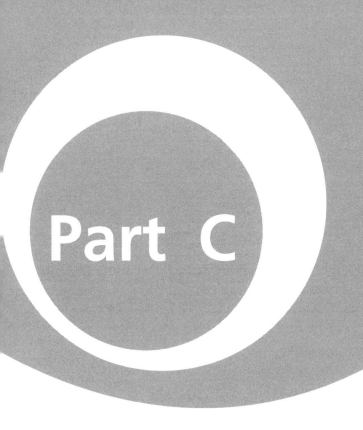

Part C

Risk and Accounting

The Role of the Management Accountant in Risk Management

Paul M. Collier* and Anthony J. Berry[†]

*Monash University, Australia
†Manchester Metropolitan University, UK

Introduction

Management accounting has been defined as the application of the principles of accounting and financial management to create, protect, preserve and increase value so as to deliver that value to stakeholders (Chartered Institute of Management Accountants, 2005). This implies at least some involvement in risk and a great deal of involvement in controls.

Management accountants, whose professional training includes the analysis of information and systems, performance and strategic management, can have a significant role to play in developing and implementing risk management and internal control systems within their organisations (Chartered Institute of Management Accountants, 2002b). In the UK, the Chartered Institute of Management Accountants (CIMA) has a final year compulsory subject – Risk and Control Strategy – that takes an integrated approach to corporate governance, risk management and internal control and a far broader accommodation of financial, non-financial quantitative and qualitative forms of control.

Scapens et al. (2003) argued that a key role for management accountants in the twenty-first century was integrating different sources of information and explaining the interconnections between non-financial performance measures and management accounting information. This would enable individual managers to see the linkages between their day-to-day operations, how these operations are presented in the management accounts, and how they link to the broader strategic concerns of the business as reflected in the non-financial measures. Although Scapens et al. did not address the management accountant's role in risk management per se, each of these roles implicitly involve accountants to a greater or lesser extent in identifying and managing risk.

This chapter proceeds by considering accounting for risk and the control of risk in the accounting and managerial tradition. Some further approaches to risk from organisational and cultural stances are also considered. Also presented are some of the findings of a recent research project on the relationship between risk management and management accounting. Risk stance was found to be a useful construct for understanding how risk management is practised.

Accounting for risk

Risk is typically considered in management accounting texts through techniques such as decision trees, probabilities, standard deviation and portfolio analysis. In contrast, finance texts consider risk in terms of hedging techniques, discount rates for the cost of capital in capital investment evaluations, and beta analysis in the capital–asset pricing model. Ruefli et al. (1999) identified two measures of risk that have predominated: the capital assets pricing model in capital markets and variance analysis, an accounting approach.

The link between accounting and risk has been recognised (Chartered Institute of Management Accountants, 2002a; International Federation of Accountants, 1999), although few studies of the relationship between risk and accounting have been carried out. Examples of recent research include risk disclosure in financial reports (Solomon et al., 2000; Linsley and Shrives, 2006), and accounting for risk in capital investment decision-making (Harris, 1999; 2000; Helliar et al., 2002).

Budgets are one of the most visible forms of risk management. Budgets are established in line with strategy and a view can be taken for each budget year as to whether the budget will contribute to achieving the strategy, a process of feed forward. Budgets also hold managers accountable for achieving financial targets (e.g. revenue, cost, profit, return on investment, etc.) by which variances between actual and budget performance must be explained and corrective action taken, a process of feedback.

Budgeting is an area where risk can be considered through sensitivity analysis. However, problems of bias (Lowe and Shaw, 1968) and aggregation (Otley and Berry, 1979) in budgeting have been recognised for many years. In their study of budgeting in four organisations, Collier and Berry (2002) found that organisational members saw risk not only in financial terms but also in terms of operational, political and personal domains, which reinforced a social construction perspective. The cases in the Collier and Berry study revealed that, by excluding some risks and considering others, the budget process was different to, and needed to be interpreted separately from, the content of the budget in which there was little evidence of any risk-modelling or the use of probabilities.

Control of risk

Internal control is the whole system of financial, human resource, operational and other controls established in order to provide reasonable assurance of effective and efficient operation, financial control, and compliance with laws and regulations. The Combined Code on Corporate Governance (Financial Reporting Council, 2003) requires that a board should maintain a sound system of internal control to safeguard shareholders' investments and the company's assets.

Traditionally, internal control has been equated with internal financial control, although the increased attention to corporate governance and enterprise risk management has shifted the agenda from a purely financial focus to a broader risk-based approach to control. This shift affects the management accountant whose role has encompassed many aspects of internal control. Internal financial controls are established to provide reasonable assurance of the safeguarding of assets against unauthorised use or disposition; the maintenance of proper accounting records; and the reliability of financial information used within the business or for publication.

Financial controls are important in all organisations. They include control over cash, debtors, inventory, fixed assets, creditors, loans, income and expenses. There are various methods by which financial control is exercised, but perhaps the main ones are budgets (see the previous section), standard costing and variance analysis, capital investment appraisal and transfer pricing. While accountants generally accept these controls, they can be criticised on a number of grounds. For example, standard costing assumes a static high volume manufacturing environment, something that is no longer a feature of Western economies. Variance analysis, like standard costing, focuses narrowly on price variations rather than overall efficiencies, particularly in JIT and TQM environments. Costs calculated for pricing and decision-making are problematic as a result of the overhead allocation problem and the Beyond Budgeting movement (Hope and Fraser, 2003) has criticised budgeting as a management tool. The desire to reduce waste, including non-productive accounting practices in lean organisations has also brought into question some of the accounting controls that accountants have come to rely on (Womack and Jones, 2003). Capital investment appraisal uses techniques that are applied to often subjective estimates of future cash flows. Capital investment decisions are often made subjectively and then justified ex post by the application of financial techniques. Transfer-pricing procedures can result in divisionalised businesses acting contrary to the corporate interest.

The emergence of greater attention to lean systems and strategic management accounting approaches such as life cycle and target costing, customer profitability analysis, supply chain and competitor analysis may also influence the value of traditional accounting tools and encourage the use of different approaches. The decline in use, or at least questioning, of some traditional accounting techniques has important implications for control purposes as accounting techniques may have a reduced role to play in future assurances about effective management control.

Further perspectives on risk

Almost all of the recent literature of risk management is in the managerialist, functionalist or positivist conception of risk. There are three limitations to this narrow perspective, often taken by accountants, of risk:

- the value of quantification techniques for measuring risk probabilistically has been questioned since the 1930s (McGoun, 1995);
- there has been a reduction of human agency to irrelevance; and
- risk has traditionally been viewed as negative and something to be avoided, despite the now-well-accepted idea of a risk/return trade-off.

The view of risk as a systematic, rational device with tools and techniques to manage risk has been challenged (Beck, 1986) (1992 in translation) with a wider view than the individual or the organisation. Beck's claim that we live in a 'risk society' was made from the stance that much risk was both part of the physical environment and also substantially created by the actions of a variety of actors – government, business, farmers, etc.

Adams (1995) has shown that everyone has a propensity to take risks, but this propensity varies from person to person, being influenced by the potential rewards of risk-taking and perceptions of risk, which are influenced by the experience of 'accidents'. Hence individual risk-taking represents a balance between perceptions of risk and the propensity to take risks. Prior research shows that we know little about how managers consider risks but we know that managers do take risks, based on risk preferences at individual and organisational levels. Some of these risk preferences vary with national culture (Weber and Hsee, 1998) organisational culture (Marshall et al., 1996) while others are individual traits (Weber and Milliman, 1997).

One implication of this cultural or social construction perspective for risk management is that the homogeneity of an organisation's management pool may well prevail, as recruitment processes deselect those whose risk preference trait is incompatible with the existing organisational preference. Simultaneously, socialisation processes may aim to normalise risk perceptions about the organisation's environment, particularly for occupational groups like accountants. Here there may be a risk of lost opportunities arising from a common organisational perspective.

Applying this broader cultural perspective, Douglas and Wildavsky (1983: 14) saw risk as a joint product of knowledge about the future and consent about the most desired prospects, identifying the perception of risk as a social process.

They commented that 'each culture, each set of shared values and supporting social institutions is biased toward highlighting certain risks and downplaying others'.

There is an important distinction here between objective, measurable risk and subjective, perceived risk. Despite the emphasis on objectivity in much writing on accounting and finance, many risks are not objectively identifiable and measurable, e.g. the risks of litigation, economic downturn, loss of key employees, natural disasters, and loss of reputation. These are all to a large extent subjective judgements. Risk is therefore to a considerable extent 'socially constructed' whereby some risks are highlighted while others are downplayed (Douglas and Wildavsky, 1983) whilst responses to risk reflect that social construction. March and Shapira (1987) noted that both individual and institutionalised risk preferences (i.e. those taken for granted within the organisation) were important in understanding organisational responses to risk management.

Risk can therefore be considered by reference to:

- the existence of internal or external events;
- information about those events (i.e. their visibility);
- managerial perception about events and information (i.e. how they are perceived); and
- how organisations establish tacit/informal or explicit/formal ways of dealing with risk.

Management accounting and risk management

This section of this chapter is based upon a survey research project to understand the relationship between risk management and management accounting (Collier et al., 2007). The survey population was management accountants (CIMA members), stock exchange listed companies (FTSE) and small- and medium-sized enterprises (SME). The analysis of the survey results was informed by interviews with members of organisations with responsibility for risk management.

Risk and governance

The survey results suggested that risk management was driven by an institutional response to calls for improved corporate governance which may reflect both protection and economic opportunity. Two external drivers of risk management practices were observed: external stakeholders, and the demands of regulators and legislation. These drivers were enacted through Boards of Directors, which were likely to exert influence over the policies and methods adopted for risk management. Further it was observed that the respondents considered that risk management was an important task for senior management, especially for CEOs, the Board and Finance Directors. The audit committee, internal audit and risk managers were scored lower while management accountants were scored at the lowest or second lowest level. Most respondents did not consider management accountants to have a significant role in risk management at all. While management accountants responded that they considered their involvement in risk management was too low, other respondents considered that it was about right. However, 42 per cent of respondents believed that the involvement of accountants in risk management was increasing. The interviewees supported the survey evidence that accountants were not central to risk management as the following two quotations illustrate:

> Management Accountant 'It's a different skill set. [Accountants] have certain skills and we have certain knowledge and that is used in a very effective way... [Risk management is] an area of expertise that you don't just step into over night, you need the in depth knowledge and understanding ... if you are looking at an organisation's financial risk then your [accountants] are better skilled in those areas. I think it is horses for courses really'

> Vice President, European federation of risk management associations. 'Management accountants don't have the skill set to drive risk management because it's about cultural change, not about banging out a new process ... the skill set for changing a culture is probably quite different to the skill set for the management accountant. It's a lot more about influencing, changing people's thinking, all those aspects of change management'

The predominant view was that accountants should be in supportive rather than a leading role in relation to risk management. It was generally agreed that management accountants had an important role to play, but this was largely concerned with producing analyses of the impact of risks to support risk managers. A likely cause of this subordinate role is the stereotypical view of accountants being risk averse.

The risk propensity of accountants

The risk propensity of accountants appeared to follow the stereotype of accountants being more risk-averse than the FTSE or SME respondents (see Figure 7.1 below), although accountants did report that they had slightly increased their willingness to take risks over the past 2 years, while other respondents reported a slight decrease in their propensity to take risks. Overall, the survey found that CIMA respondents were more risk-concerned than the other respondent groups in relation to their organisations, despite having a lower perception of competitive intensity and uncertainty in their industry/sector.

Management accountants and their organisations

Table 7.1 shows that 24 per cent of CIMA members were at considerable variance to their organisations. Those in the upper right and lower left cells were either willing to take risks but saw their organisations as risk averse, or risk averse but saw their organisations as willing to take risks. 47 per cent of

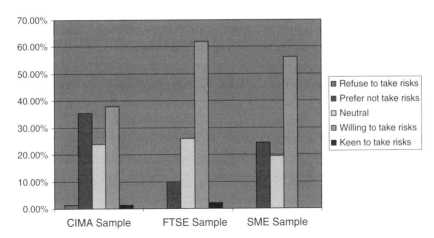

Figure 7.1 Propensity to take risks

Table 7.1 Comparison of personal and organisational risk appetite for CIMA members

| | | Organisational risk appetite | | |
		Risk Averse	Risk neutral	Risk willing
Personal risk appetite	Risk averse	22%	5%	10%
	Risk neutral	9%	6%	9%
	Risk willing	14%	6%	19%

CIMA members took the same attitude to risk as they saw their organisations taking, whilst 29 per cent had some lesser degree of mismatch.

Interestingly, the mismatch was greater for the CIMA respondents than for the other two survey groups (FTSE and SME). This may explain the reasons why management accountants were reported as having a low level of responsibility for elements of risk management and may also be a reason why other respondents did not wish to increase the role of management accountants in risk management.

Integration of management accounting and risk management systems

As described above, management accountants typically have a considerable responsibility for designing, implementing and monitoring control systems, many of which are in relation to risk, albeit predominantly financial risk. The survey asked CIMA members whether their accounting and risk management systems were integrated. Only about a quarter of the respondents reported any degree of integration of systems while two-fifths of respondents reported a lack of integration.

Methods of risk management in use

The survey classified methods of risk management as subjective, basic and technical, as shown in Table 7.2 'Those in the upper right and lower ... risk averse, or risk averse but saw their organisations as willing to take risks.'

Table 7.2 Categories of risk management methods

Subjective methods of risk management	Basic methods of risk management	Technical methods of risk management
Experience, intuition, hindsight and judgement	Brainstorming, scenario analysis, PEST/SWOT analysis Interviews, surveys, questionnaires Likelihood/ consequences matrix Monitoring using a risk register or written reports	Stochastic modelling, statistical analysis Risk management software

The methods of risk management in highest use were the more subjective ones (particularly experience, intuition and hindsight), with quantitative methods used least of all. However, compared to the CIMA accountants, a higher proportion of FTSE and SME respondents believed that risk management in their organisations was handled through a formal control system.

The survey results suggested that CIMA respondents may have had less confidence than other respondents in the use of control systems for risk management purposes. One interviewee explained this:

> It is very difficult to get a solid database on which to start doing quantitative analysis you know, the world changes and all the factors change, so it is very difficult to start putting figures on . . . I think it's very intuitive, in that you learn as you go along and the only way you can do that is on past experience and therefore the more experience you can tap into, the better your intuition can become . . .

Group Risk Manager, FTSE company, Financial Services.

Overall, the research results suggested that subjective or heuristic approaches may be more important and more useful for risk management than systematic procedures.

Risk management and culture

Respondents were invited to assess the extent to which their organisation had a range of processes and a culture to support risk management and internal control. Overall, more than half of the respondents were satisfied with the supportive risk management processes and internal control systems. However, only about half of the respondents felt that in their organisation risks were understood and embedded at the cultural level.

Changes in risk management approaches

Reported changes in the approach to risk management in the past, present and future are summarised in Figure 7.2. This reflects the respondents' experience that risk had shifted from being considered tacitly in the past to being considered more formally in the present, and their expectation that this trend would shift markedly in the future to a more holistic approach with risk being used to aid decision-making. All survey groups (including CIMA) reflected a similar

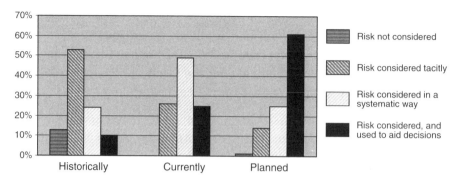

Figure 7.2 Trends in risk management

trend to that shown in Figure 7.2. The expected reduction in significance of the systematic approaches was accompanied by a clear expectation of a future decision focus.

Benefits of risk management

Risk management may be seen largely as an exercise in compliance with corporate governance requirements. However, half of the respondents reported that the benefits exceeded the costs, with 40 per cent reporting that benefits and costs were neutral. The accountants were less confident than others surveyed that risk management had led to improved reporting (Table 7.3).

Although the difference was not so significant, accountants were a little less confident than other respondents that risk management had improved their organisations' allocation and utilisation of resources (Table 7.4).

Table 7.3 To what degree has risk management improved your organisation's management reporting?

	No improvement		Some improvement		Significant improvement
	1	2	3	4	5
Total sample	9.1%	16.9%	39.2%	29.2%	5.6%
CIMA sample	10.5%	19.2%	40.1%	25.8%	4.4%

Table 7.4 To what degree has risk management improved your organisation's resource allocation and utilisation?

	No improvement		Some improvement		Significant improvement
	1	2	3	4	5
Total sample	9.7%	24.1%	42.4%	21.3%	2.5%
CIMA sample	10.5%	24.0%	41.1%	22.7%	1.7%

Risk stance: A framework for understanding

The results of the research reported above suggested that although management accountants wanted a greater involvement in risk, non-financial managers did not support this, citing the different skill set needed. The risk propensity of accountants was lower than that for FTSE and SME respondents and the degree of mismatch between their personal risk propensity and that of their organisations was greater than that for the other respondents. Heuristic, rather than more formal methods of risk management seemed to be preferred, whilst management accountants had less confidence in the formal systems than their non-accounting colleagues. Accountants were also less confident in those systems improving financial reporting and resourcing decisions. The research found that the socially constructed view of risk was a better reflection of organisational risk management than rational modelling approaches typified by textbooks and professional training. This view reflects the subjectivity of risk perceptions and preferences, cultural constraints and individual traits.

Douglas and Wildavsky (1983) argued for some basic constructions of risk based upon two dimensions: the degree of equality (how choice is negotiated or constrained), and the degree of individualism/collectivism. Following Douglas and Wildavsky, Adams (1995) identified four 'rationalities' that have an impact on risk. These were: Fatalists, Hierarchists, Individualists and Egalitarians.

Fatalists have minimal control over their own lives and belong to no groups that are responsible for the decisions that rule their lives. They are resigned to their fate and see no point in trying to change it, so risk management is irrelevant to Fatalists. Hierarchists inhabit a world with strong group boundaries and social relationships that are hierarchical. Hierarchists are always evident in large organisations with strong structures, procedures and systems. They are most comfortable with a bureaucratic risk management system using various risk management techniques. Individualists are enterprising, self-made people, relatively free from control by others, but who strive to exert control over their environment. Entrepreneurs in small–medium enterprises fit into this category. Risk management to Individualists is typically intuitive rather than systematic. Egalitarians have strong group loyalties but little respect for externally imposed rules and group decisions are arrived at democratically. Egalitarians are more commonly found in public sector and not-for-profit organisations whose values are oriented to social rather than economic concerns. Egalitarians are most comfortable in situations of risk sharing through insurance, hedging or transfer to other organisations.

Based on the survey respondents' views as to whether risk management in their organisations was largely about avoiding negative consequences or achieving positive consequences, Figure 7.3 presents an adaptation from the four ideal types of Adams which we describe as an organisational 'risk stance'.

The Risk Sceptical (Adams' Fatalists) are those who do not see risk management as being important or having any consequences, or who were neutral in their view. This group comprised only 7 per cent of the respondents. Entrepreneurs (Adams' Individualists) agreed that risk management was about positive consequences but disagreed or were neutral about negative consequences, perhaps reflecting their status as a risk-seeking group. 14 per cent of respondents fitted this category. Hierarchists disagreed or were neutral in relation to positive consequences but agreed in relation to negative ones. This is the risk-avoiding group, representing 36 per cent of respondents. The Risk Aware group (Adams' Egalitarians) were balanced between risk management's role in both achieving positive and avoiding negative consequences. 43 per cent of the respondents could be classified as Risk Aware. The Risk Aware group would be likely to embed risk in culture and decision-making.

		RM is about achieving positive consequences	
		Disagree/Neutral	Agree
RM is about avoiding negative consequences	Disagree/Neutral	Risk sceptical 7%	Entrepreneurs 14%
	Agree	Hierarchists 36%	Risk aware 43%

Figure 7.3 Classification of risk management responses by risk stance (*Source*: Adapted from Adams (1995) and Douglas and Wildavsky (1983))

The four risk stances – Risk Sceptical, Entrepreneurs, Hierarchists and Risk Aware – are a means of exploring and understanding individual and organisational risk management practices.

The impact of risk stance

The research survey results suggested that risk stance had a significant moderating influence on methods of risk management (whether heuristic or systematic approaches were adopted). Risk management is mostly conceived of as fitting a Hierarchist stance in respect of methods of risk management and a process stance in respect of the Risk Aware organisations.

There were two process variables that supported the risk management methods. The first was the degree to which there were supporting policies and culture, the second was the degree to which risks were factored into plans.

Hierarchists exhibited strong positive correlations between the degree of supporting policies and culture and the use of basic and technical risk management methods. There were also strong positive correlations of risk management methods with the degree of reported improved performance and improved external relationships.

The Risk Aware group similarly showed strong positive correlations of the degree of supporting policies and culture with the degree of use of basic and technical risk management methods. For the Risk Aware group, there were also strong positive correlations of the degree of risk being factored into organisational planning and the degrees of improved performance and improved external relationships.

For Entrepreneurs, there were weaker positive correlations of the process variables supporting policies and culture with the use of basic and technical risk management methods. The strongest positive correlations were between the risk management methods and improvements to external relationships.

For the Risk Sceptical, there were even fewer correlations. There was no correlation between supporting policies and culture and the use of basic and technical risk management methods. There was some weak positive correlation between risks being factored into organisational planning, risk management having improved organisational performance and having improved external relationships.

Risk of control

Earlier in this chapter it was suggested that there was a risk arising from the possible drift towards homogeneity of personnel attitudes to risk. The control of risk has been contrasted with a different problem, the risk arising from control (Berry et al., 2005). There is an implicit assumption in corporate governance approaches that the higher the risk (in terms of likelihood and consequences), the higher must be the control of that risk. However, this is a circular argument. Risk is deemed to be high because something is either uncertain or has significant consequences, or both. If the likelihood and consequence of risks could be controlled, then by definition they would not be considered risky. This is a parallel argument to that made by the 'Beyond Budgeting' movement.

While risk management techniques may be effective for risks over which the organisation has control, external risks are a different matter. Organisations can develop methods of anticipation, prepare contingency plans and adapt to flexible practices but in those cases 'control' may impede or prevent anticipation, contingency and flexibility. This is the first risk of control: the lack of flexibility.

As perceptions of, and attitudes toward, risk vary, the risk of control is that controls are implemented – following the Turnbull/Combined Code recommendation for a 'risk-based approach' to establishing a system of internal control – to provide against worst-case scenarios. But these controls may prevent opportunities from being grasped. Controls may become more prescriptive and more dependent on the predictive model used such that organisational actions are overly constrained. Consequently, organisational participants may have less 'room to manoeuvre' and in a turbulent environment this may result in an increase, rather than a decrease, in risk as policies, plans and budgets do not have the flexibility to cope with the unexpected. This is the second risk of control: the refusal of opportunity.

Excessive control, in order to ensure compliance with corporate governance, can over-focus on downside risk and result in opportunities being missed. This is not an argument for a lack of control, but for the appropriate application of sensible controls that permit flexibility of response in the light of emerging trends and unexpected environmental changes.

Applying the approach to risk stance described in the previous section, we can identify the risk of control through control systems that have unreliable predictive models (relied on by Hierarchists), or systems of control that are dependent on differing perceptions among individuals (ignored by Entrepreneurs). The risk of control can constrain the ability to cope (relied on by the Risk Aware) or adopt the position that risk cannot be managed or controlled at all (the Risk Sceptical position). This presents a dilemma for managers who seek to manage and control risk.

Conclusion

This chapter has reviewed accounting and risk management and their relationship. Much risk management was found to be based upon the requirements of corporate governance to demonstrate risk management and internal control policies and practices in order to obtain institutional legitimacy. However, from the research project (Collier et al., 2007) while (hierarchic) systems and processes need to be in place to ensure that gaps and overlaps in risk management are avoided, the (risk aware) cultural approach is to recognise the socially constructed nature of risk propensity and risk perception, while the (entrepreneurial) perspective needs to be encouraged in a spirit of anticipation, contingency and flexibility where controls encourage and empower, rather than constrain behaviour that is sensitive to the risk–return trade-off.

This chapter has considered the arguments for a greater involvement by management accountants in risk management. However, it is clear that certain impediments exist to such an expanded role, including the high risk aversion of accountants, the reliability of risk management controls and the risk stance adopted by the organisation.

Acknowledgements

The authors acknowledge the financial support of the Chartered Institute of Management Accountants (CIMA) in the conduct of this research and for the advice provided by the Association of Insurance and Risk Managers (AIRMIC). A full copy of the research report is in Collier, P.M., Berry, A.J. and Burke, G.T. (2007). *Risk and Management Accounting: Best Practice Guidelines for Enterprise-wide Internal Control Procedures*. Oxford, Elsevier.

References

Adams, J. (1995). *Risk*. UCL Press, London.
Beck, U. (1986) (1992, in translation). *Risk Society*. Sage, London.

Berry, A.J., Collier, P.M., Helliar, C.V. et al. (2005). 'Risk and Control: The Control of Risk and the Risk of Control', in Berry, A.J., Broadbent, J. and Otley, D. (eds) *Management Control: Theories, Issues and Performance*. Palgrave Macmillan, Basingstoke, pp. 279–299.

Chartered Institute of Management Accountants (2002a). *Managing Risk to Enhance Stakeholder Value: CIMA & IFAC Financial and Management Accounting Committee*, IFAC, New York.

Chartered Institute of Management Accountants (2002b). *Risk Management: A Guide to Good Practice*. CIMA Publishing, London.

Chartered Institute of Management Accountants (2005). *CIMA Official Terminology: 2005 Edition*. Elsevier, Oxford.

Collier, P.M. and Berry, A.J. (2002). 'Risk in the Process of Budgeting', *Management Accounting Research*, Vol. 13, pp. 273–297.

Collier, P.M., Berry, A.J. and Burke, G.T. (2007). *Risk and Management Accounting: Best Practice Guidelines for Enterprise-Wide Internal Control Procedures*. Elsevier, Oxford.

Douglas, M. and Wildavsky, A. (1983). *Risk and Culture: An Essay on the Selection of Technological and Environmental Dangers*. University of California Press, Berkeley, CA.

Financial Reporting Council (2003). The Combined Code on Corporate Governance, London.

Harris, E.P. (1999). 'Project Risk Assessment: A European Field Study', *British Accounting Review*, Vol. 31, pp. 347–371.

Harris, E.P. (2000). 'Strategic Investment Decision-Making: Managerial Judgement on Project Risk and Return', *Journal of Applied Accounting Research*, Vol. 5, pp. 87–110.

Helliar, C.V., Lomie, A.A., Power, D.M. and Sinclair, C.D. (2002). 'Managerial Attitudes to risk: A Comparison of Scottish Chartered Accountants and U.K. Managers', *Journal of International Accounting, Auditing & Taxation*, Vol. 11, pp. 156–190.

Hope, J. and Fraser, R. (2003). *Beyond Budgeting: How Managers can Break Free from the Annual Performance Trap*. Harvard Business School Press, Boston, MA.

International Federation of Accountants (1999). 'Enhancing Shareholder Wealth by Better Managing Business Risk', *International Management Accounting Study, No. 9*, New York.

Linsley, P.M. and Shrives, P.J. (2006). 'Risk Reporting: A Study of Risk Disclosures in the Annual Reports of UK Companies', *British Accounting Review*, Vol. 38, pp. 387–404.

Lowe, E.A. and Shaw, R.W. (1968). 'An Analysis of Managerial Biasing: Evidence from a Company's Budgeting Process', *Journal of Management Studies*, October, pp. 304–315.

March, J.G. and Shapira, Z. (1987). 'Managerial Perspectives on Risk and Risk Taking', *Management Science*, Vol. 33, pp. 1404–1418.

Marshall, C., Prusak, L. and Shpilberg, D. (1996). 'Financial Risk and the Need for Superior Knowledge Management', *California Management Review*, Vol. 38, pp. 77–101.

McGoun, E.G. (1995). 'The History of Risk "Measurement"', *Critical Perspectives on Accounting*, Vol. 6, pp. 511–532.

Otley, D. and Berry, A. (1979). 'Risk Distribution in the Budgetary Process', *Accounting and Business Research*, Vol. 9, pp. 325–327.

Ruefli, T.W., Collins, J.M. and Lacugna, J.R. (1999). 'Risk Measures in Strategic Management: Auld Lang Syne?', *Strategic Management Journal*, Vol. 20, pp. 167–194.

Scapens, R.W., Ezzamel, M., Burns, J. and Baldvinsdottir, G. (2003). *The Future Direction of UK Management Accounting Practice*. Elsevier, Oxford.

Solomon, J.F., Solomon, A., Norton, S.D. et al. (2000). 'A Conceptual Framework for Corporate Risk Disclosure Emerging from the Agenda for Corporate Governance Reform', *British Accounting Review*, Vol. 32, pp. 447–478.

Weber, E.U. and Hsee, C. (1998). 'Cross-cultural Differences in Risk Perception, but Cross-cultural Similarities in Attitudes Towards Perceived Risk', *Management Science*, Vol. 44, pp. 1205–1217.

Weber, E.U. and Milliman, R.A. (1997). 'Perceived Risk Attitudes: Relating Risk Perception to Risky Choice', *Management Science*, Vol. 43, pp. 123–144.

Womack, J.P. and Jones, D.T. (2003). *Lean Thinking: Banish Waste and Create Wealth in your Corporation*. Free Press, London.

Financial Risk Management

Christine Helliar

University of Dundee, UK

Introduction

This book examines risk from several different viewpoints and from a number of different perspectives in order to address the various risks that are faced in different organisations. The current chapter examines financial risks to which nearly all organisations are exposed. These financial risks derive from exposure to interest rates, foreign exchange rates, commodity prices and/or equity prices.

Interest rate risk arises because many companies have debt financing in their capital structure, either through the issue of bonds or the use of bank debt. Other companies may hold surplus cash in the form of interest-paying investments. Interest rate risk is the exposure to movements in interest rates on these interest-bearing assets or liabilities.

Foreign exchange rate risk takes three forms. The first is transactional risk where, for example, import or export cash flows need to be managed. Translational risk is where the financial statements of overseas subsidiaries or operations are consolidated into the group financial statements. Economic risk is more nebulous and relates to the potential for future exchange rates to change the fundamental business operations of a company.

Commodity price risk affects many organisations around the world because most of them use oil, electricity or other forms of energy; as the price of energy escalates, this can have serious consequences for businesses. For example, utility companies or airlines would be particularly exposed to changes in energy prices. Other organisations may be exposed to the changes in prices of different commodities, such as metal for car manufacturers, or agricultural product prices for food-processing businesses.

Equity price risk affects any individual or institution that invests in the shares of quoted companies. As share prices rise or fall, the shareholdings will earn gains or make losses. Changes in share prices may affect the potential merger or acquisition of a company, the solvency of a pension fund, the performance of an investment trust or the absolute returns of a hedge fund.

Nearly all organisations face at least one of these four exposures, and many will experience several of them. Most companies, therefore, adopt a financial risk management programme, known as hedging, to reduce these inherent financial risks within their business. The two most common risks that are hedged by companies are interest rate risk and exchange rate risk. The rest of this chapter concentrates on these two risks in particular.

Hedging

Hedging is a strategy in which a financial risk is eliminated or reduced by passing the risk on to someone else; this activity is usually conducted by corporate treasurers when managing their companies' financial risks. However, the level of hedging that treasurers undertake depends on their firms' attitudes to risk. Some organisations may choose not to hedge their exposures, others may hedge all of their financial risks. In their study of foreign exchange risk management, Belk and Glaum (1990) found that managers in 9 of the 16 companies they visited were initially classified as risk averse and only three managers appeared to be risk-seeking. However, on further investigation, the staff in only three of the companies that they visited appeared to be truly risk averse. They concluded that:

> Only a minority were risk averse in the full meaning of the term. The majority to varying degrees accepted the risks inherent in uncovered foreign exchange exposures, or even sought to increase these risks in order to profit from their foreign exchange risk management. (p. 11).

Thus, the management of risk depends upon the risk appetite of managers and their views on the direction in which rates or prices are likely to go in the future. In general, large companies tend to actively manage their financial exposures and adopt a hedging programme by transacting in derivative products known as forwards, futures, options and swaps.

Forwards

Forwards are useful for hedging a known transaction that will occur in the short to medium term, such as in 3 months' time. There are two types of forward contracts: forward rate agreements and foreign exchange forward contracts.

Forward rate agreements

A forward rate agreement (FRA) is the product used to hedge interest rate risk and is an agreement whereby an organisation can lock into an interest rate today for a period of time starting in the future. On the future date the two counterparties in the FRA settle up and, depending upon the direction of interest rates, one will pay an amount of money to the other representing the difference between the FRA rate and the actual rate, as shown in Example 8.1.

Example 8.1

A company has a £100 million loan where the interest rate is reset every year for the following year, and the interest is payable at the end of that period. If rates today are 5.5 per cent, with 6 months to go before the annual reset date, the treasurer may decide that interest rates are likely to rise to 6 per cent and may wish to fix the rate on the next year's interest rate in 6 months' time at 5.5 per cent and pay £5.5 million in interest. By entering into an FRA the treasurer locks in a rate today. If interest rates rise, say to 6 per cent, the treasurer saves the organisation £0.5 million. However, if interest rates do not rise but fall, the company will have to pay more in interest payments than might otherwise be necessary as it is locked into the rate of 5.5 per cent. However, this outcome would not be known until 6 months' time at the beginning of the yearly interest period. In effect, in 6 months' time the company either receives the £0.5 million saving, or pays the excess over current lower rates.

Foreign exchange forward contracts

A foreign exchange forward contract is similar to a forward rate agreement for interest rates. A foreign exchange forward allows an enterprise to buy or sell a fixed amount of currency at some date in the future at a pre-determined price. With an FRA only the net difference between the agreed interest rate and the actual interest rate amount is paid by one party to the other. However, with a foreign exchange forward the whole amount of each currency is exchanged, as shown in Example 8.2.

Example 8.2

An exporter in the UK agrees to sell goods to a German company today for Euro 1 million and the spot (current) exchange rate is GBP/EUR 1.40 at the time of the sale. Thus, the exporter expects to receive £714 286. If the exporter does not expect to receive payment for the goods for 3 months, the exchange rate may fluctuate between the agreed date of sale and the receipt of the Euros. If the Euro strengthens against the pound to GBP/EUR

1.30, the exporter will receive £769 231. If however the Euro weakens against the pound to GBP/EUR 1.50 then the exporter will only receive £666 667. To avoid the uncertainty of the final sterling receipt the exporter could hedge the exchange rate risk by taking out a foreign exchange forward contract. On the day the sale is agreed, a foreign exchange forward contract could be taken out to exchange the Euro 1 million for pounds sterling at a pre-determined rate set at that time. If the 3-month forward rate is GBP/EUR 1.40 the exporter has locked in a sterling amount today for the Euros receivable in 3 months' time of £714 286. Whatever happens to the exchange rate between the day the forward contract is agreed and the future date when the proceeds are received, the exporter knows that £714 286 will be received in exchange for the Euro 1 million.

Futures

Interest rate futures

Futures are similar to forwards but are institutionalised forms of forwards traded on recognised exchanges; both FRAs and futures 'lock in' a price today for a transaction that will occur at some time in the future. FRAs are normally transacted with banks and other financial institutions, and are tailored to suit the dates and amounts that a company requires. However, interest rate futures are transacted on the floor of an exchange and each contract is for a pre-specified amount on a pre-specified date; this relative inflexibility may not suit all organisations. Examples of USD interest rate futures, which are the most actively traded, are Eurodollar futures contracts, T-bond futures contracts and T-bill futures contracts. Apart from the inflexibility of contract amounts and dates a further problem is that they are difficult to administer because of the daily margin payments which are required by the exchange on which futures are traded; many organisations find these calculations and payments burdensome. However, futures contracts are very liquid since an active market exists for these products and most firms find them easy to liquidate. This is not the case with FRAs. With an FRA, if a company changes its view on interest rates, it cannot sell the FRA contract but has to take out a second FRA to reverse the obligations embedded in the first FRA. With a future it is a very easy matter to just sell the instrument. In practice, however, many organisations use FRAs, but relatively few use futures (Helliar, 1997) because of the inflexibility and administration requirements.

Foreign exchange futures

A foreign exchange futures contract is similar to a foreign exchange forward contract, and Example 8.2 (above) of the forward foreign exchange contract can also be used as an example of how futures can be used by firms as it has the same monetary outcome. However, like interest rate futures, foreign exchange futures contracts are traded on an exchange and are for set dates and pre-determined quantities of currencies. Because there are only set dates for futures contracts, normally every 3 months in March, June, September and December, the exporter cannot hedge for a specific date, say 27 April, and may have to use a proportion of March and June futures contracts to mimic an exposure to late April. As with interest rate futures, foreign exchange futures encounter the same administrative difficulties. Table 8.1 illustrates some of the main differences between using forwards and futures.

The use of both forwards and futures has exactly the same effect of locking in an exchange rate today for a pre-determined amount at a pre-determined price on a fixed date in the future. However, each product has its advantages and disadvantages. Forwards are good for companies that need precise amounts on odd dates or for odd amounts or exotic (unusual) currencies, such as the Botswana Pula. Forwards are also better from an administrative point of view

Table 8.1 A comparison of forwards and futures for currencies

Forwards	Futures
Over-the-counter	Exchange traded
Tailor made	Structured by the Exchange
Any date	Only set dates, March, June, September and December
Any amount	Only pre-determined contract amounts
Illiquid	Liquid
Credit risk with counterparty	Low credit risk
One payment date	Daily variation margin payments
Any currencies	Only major currencies

as there is no requirement to pay gains or losses on a daily basis. However, there is very little credit risk with futures, as each transaction is deemed to be done with the exchange and the daily variation margin payments representing losses and profits on the contracts ensure that there are never any unrealised profits that have not yet been paid in cash. Futures contracts are also very easy to unwind as they are easy to buy and sell. In practice most commercial organisations use forwards and most financial institutions use futures. Both, though, are very efficient hedging tools.

Options

Interest rate options

An option is the right, but not the obligation, to carry out a transaction at some time in the future for a price which is established today. Swaps, FRAs and futures are all contracts where two parties agree to a transaction and there is a contractual obligation to carry out the terms of the agreement. However, an option gives the option buyer the choice of whether to undertake the transaction or not. A company would generally buy an option from an option seller or option writer. An option is a form of insurance, and as such an upfront premium is paid at the time when the option is taken out. Many organisations dislike paying these premiums for something that they may not want and many treasurers consider that option premiums are too expensive, as with the perception of the premiums on insurance contracts (Helliar, 1997). A number of companies now also use 'swaptions', which are options on transacting a swap at a future time which some companies also find useful.

Foreign currency options

A foreign exchange option also gives the holder of the option the right, but not the obligation, to buy or sell a designated quantity of foreign currency at a specific price during a specified period. As with interest rate options, a foreign exchange option is like an insurance policy, and as such a premium is paid up-front for the option, as shown in Example 8.3. Options are very useful hedging instruments, but they can be very expensive, depending upon the time of expiry, the strike price which is the price at which the contract will be transacted, and the underlying volatility of the exchange rate

Options are especially useful in the situation of a tender for a large overseas contract, where the outcome of the tender may not be known for, say, 6 months

---

Example 8.3

As in Example 8.2, an exporter in the UK agrees to sell goods to a German company today for Euro 1 million and the spot (current) exchange rate is GBP/EUR 1.40 at the time of the sale. The UK exporter can take out an option instead of a forward or futures contract. The exporter could purchase an option with a strike price of GBP/EUR 1.40, expiring on 27 April costing a premium of, say, £10 000. If, on 27 April, the exchange rate is GBP/EUR 1.30 the exporter will let the option lapse and will transact a spot rate transaction converting the Euros 1 million into £769 231 at the £/DM 1.30 rate (Euro 1 million/1.30). The exporter has paid the £10 000 premium though, which will result in the exporter receiving a net amount of £759 231. If the exporter has transacted a forward or a future at 1.40 only £714 286 (Euro1 million/1.40) will be received. By using an option the exporter has been able to take advantage from the upside movement of the currency. However, if the exchange rate moves to GBP/EUR 1.50, the exporter will exercise the option entitling the exporter to receive an effective rate of GBP/EUR 1.40, and receive £714 286. Deducting the cost of the option leaves the exporter with £704 286, which is less than with a forward or future because of the expense of the option premium.

---

in the future. In a tender for overseas work, if the tender is successful the final profitability of the contract may depend upon exchange rate movements. If the bid is unsuccessful, hedging is not required as there will not be any exposure to that exchange rate. An option is useful in that it gives the company making the tender the option to hedge against the exchange rate, or to not do so if the contract is lost to a competitor. Table 8.2 shows the sterling proceeds from each scenario of using forward, futures and options on £1 million against Euros.

Table 8.2 Hedging outcomes

Exchange rate	Forward@ 1.40	Future @1.40	Option @1.40	No hedge
1.30	£714 286	£714 286	£759 231	£769 231
1.40	£714 286	£714 286	£704 286	£714 286
1.50	£714 286	£714 286	£704 286	£666 667

Swaps

Interest rate swaps

An interest rate swap involves the exchange of one stream of cash flows at one interest rate for another stream of cash flows at another interest rate. For example, a company may have obtained funding through the issue of a 10-year 6.5 per cent fixed interest debenture 3 years ago. It may now be more appropriate to pay an interest rate based on current market rates (usually LIBOR which is the current rate prevailing in London known as the London Interbank Offer Rate). Instead of redeeming the debenture (if indeed this were possible) and obtaining floating rate financing, it could just undertake a 7-year (10 years– 3 years) swap (see Figure 8.1). The fixed rate side of the swap would match the 6.5 per cent rate on the debenture and the floating rate leg of the swap would represent the current short-term rates plus a credit spread and also reflect the difference between the fixed rate (6.5 per cent) and current long-term rates. Sometimes a payment is made at the start of the swap to reflect the amount by which the fixed rate leg of the swap is 'off-market'. Thus the company can synthetically manufacture for itself a 7-year loan paying current market interest rates. It is often much cheaper and easier to do a swap than to redeem existing debt and arrange new credit lines.

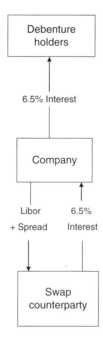

Figure 8.1 Interest rate swap

Currency swaps

Currency swaps are also useful for medium- to long-term hedging; futures, forwards and options are generally only suitable for hedging 1 or 2 years into the future. A currency swap, as its name suggests, is the exchange of principal and interest in one currency for that in another currency. The nature of the swap is most readily explained with the help of an example. Suppose that a UK company has raised finance by negotiating a £10 million 5-year loan to set up a new subsidiary in France, as in Figure 8.2. On receipt of the £10 million the company needs to convert its pounds into Euros for use in France. While the future earnings of the French subsidiary will be in Euros, the loan interest payments will still be in sterling. If the company enters a 5-year currency swap agreement at an exchange rate of £1 to Euros 1.40, the UK company will pay the swaps counterparty £10 million and receive in return Euros 14 million. Over the life of the swap the UK company will pay interest in Euros to the swap counterparty and receive UK sterling in return. This sterling can then be used to pay the interest on the original £10 million loan to the UK lender (see Figure 8.3).

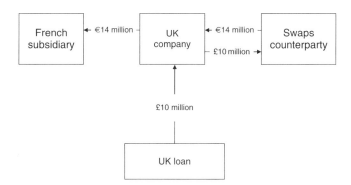

Figure 8.2 Principal payments

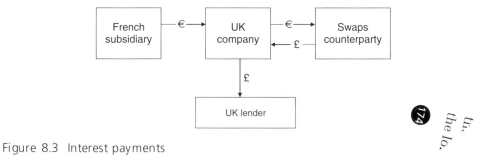

Figure 8.3 Interest payments

On maturity of the swap the £10 million and Euros 14 million would be re-exchanged. Thus, by entering into a swap agreement the UK company can obtain its required Euro funding and also match its future earnings stream to its financing costs. The swaps counterparty has taken on the exchange rate risk from the company over the life of the loan (and the swap). A company can therefore raise finance in any particular currency that it chooses and then use the swaps market to obtain the required funding in the currency that it needs.

These four types of products, swaps, options, futures and forwards are used by financial managers to actively manage their organisations' financial risks. There has been a great deal of debate about whether companies should hedge their financial risks and whether hedging adds value to an organisation. The next section discusses whether companies should use these products and hedge.

The rationale for corporate risk management and hedging

Mian (1996) defines hedging as 'the activities undertaken by the firm in order to mitigate the impact of . . . uncertainties on the value of the firm' (p. 419). This definition is the same basis as Froot, Scharfstein and Stein's (1994) analysis of the topic. They illustrate the main benefits of hedging by drawing on the biblical story of the Pharaoh and Joseph: during the 7 years of plenty the people stored food and grain and when the 7 years of famine arrived, they used these reserves and had enough food to survive. Hedging can therefore be viewed as a continuous response by risk-averse individuals to the uncertain economic future that their companies face.

However, the early finance literature argued that companies did not need to manage their risks or hedge their exposures. For example, Modigliani and Miller (1958) argued that whatever a company could do, investors could replicate. Therefore, if a company was exposed to exchange rate or interest rate risk, this exposure did not need to be hedged by the company since investors could do this for themselves. In addition, Holland (1993) argued that, over the long term, hedging might not be necessary if the expected value of the gains and losses were calculated to be zero. However, it would be little consolation if the timing of a large foreign currency receivable coincided with a large negative change in the exchange rate to know that it would correct itself with an equivalent gain in the long run. If the markets were efficient, and reflected all known information all the time, there would be no need to hedge, as hedging would be irrelevant from an efficient market perspective. But, in practice, companies might need to consider tax regimes, unexpected changes in interest rates, inflation rates and exchange rates as well as changes in their own operations.

However, in reality, risk management is widely used by finance directors, corporate treasurers and portfolio managers to reduce the volatility of their firm's reported profit. Seven reasons have been advanced in the literature to explain why companies hedge their exposures, and it is now recognised that companies employ specialist staff to conduct hedging operations (Helliar, 1997). These seven reasons are as follows.

1. *To reduce bankruptcy costs and lower the likelihood of financial distress* (Stultz, 1996). Financial distress might not necessarily mean bankruptcy, but it might increase the operating costs of the firm since no credit might be available from suppliers and loans might only be offered at a higher rate of interest. In addition, customers might demand service agreements or warranties, and the wages paid to retain employees might need to rise. Stultz (1996) argued that the goal for risk management was not variance minimisation but the elimination of costly 'lower-tail' or negative outcomes; treasurers could reduce the expected costs of financial trouble while preserving the company's ability to exploit any possible advantages in upside risk potential that it might possibly face. Hedging also improved the confidence of various stakeholder groups in the firm including customers (Eckl and Robinson, 1990).

2. *To minimise variability in cash flows* (Froot et al., 1993). Smith and Stultz (1985) indicated that hedging minimised cash flow volatility, thus reducing the probability of defaulting on financial obligations and decreasing the costs of financial distress.

3. *To reduce the impact of capital market imperfections.* Froot et al. (1993) state that risk management is ranked by financial executives as one of their most important objectives. Optimal risk management strategies build upon capital market imperfections. If imperfections make externally obtained funds more expensive than those generated internally, they can supply a rationale for risk management. Sercu and Uppal (1995) argued that firms and individuals do not have the same access to financial markets; for example, individuals are not able to participate in the forward currency market while companies have better hedging opportunities than individuals.

4. *To take advantage of economies of scale* (Mian, 1996). Nance et al. (1993) suggested that there were scale economies in the costs associated with derivatives transactions which would make it cheaper for larger firms to hedge. Large companies could take advantage of these economies of scale; they would be more likely to employ professional managers who would be familiar with hedging than the non-specialist financial staff in smaller firms.

5. *To protect managerial self-interest.* Froot, Scharfstein and Stein (1993) proposed that the labour market revised its opinions about managers' ability based on the performance of the company where they worked. By hedging, executives could smooth the earnings of the company and influence the labour market's perception of their talents. Stultz (1984) also argued that it was the managers who decided upon hedging policy, not shareholders, and that managers might hedge to maximise their expected lifetime utility by reducing the possibility that they might be compelled to leave the firm. Managers could not diversify the unique risk which was specific to their organisation since they tended not to have a diversified portfolio of investments; but instead had a large proportion of their human capital tied up in the one firm.[1] Therefore, they focused on the total risk of the enterprise and not just the market risk. Tufano (1998) also suggested that the risk being managed was that of 'career or employment risk' while Eckl and Robinson (1990) arrived at the same conclusion but from the viewpoint of the firm; they suggested that hedging could reduce the costs associated with hiring and firing staff when an organisation had volatile earnings.

6. *To lower tax payments or allow regulatory arbitrage* (Rawls and Smithson, 1990). Companies often have a convex tax function, such that, as income rises, the tax rate increases also. It may, therefore, be more efficient to try and smooth each year's earnings through hedging so that higher tax rates are not levied on any year's profits; companies can hedge to ensure that the same tax rate is maintained in consecutive years. A similar argument can be made for regulatory arbitrage – an argument suggested by Smith and Stultz (1985) and Eckl and Robinson (1990). Companies may actively engage in trying to avoid regulatory hurdles such as the excessive costs incurred when raising new finance by obtaining funding

---

[1] For example, Gilson (1989) found that none of the CEOs from the Fortune 500 firms who had lost their jobs because their companies got into financial distress were ever employed as executives in other Fortune 500 firms.

in a market other than the domestic market. Thus, a company based in the US may raise funds through the Euromarkets in a currency other than dollars and then hedge the mismatch in currency flows.

7. *To improve investment decisions* (Froot et al., 1994). Modigliani and Miller suggested that companies did not need to hedge because value was only created when companies made positive net present value investments; the choice of funding had no impact on the value of the firm. However, Froot et al. (1994) pointed out that companies needed to predict what their cash flows would be in order to be able to make these investments. If an organisation knew the amount of funds that would be available it would be able to plan its capital spending programme and earn the expected net present value of these investments. If a company was not able to plan ahead it might invest in less efficient assets and ultimately earn a lower rate of return. Essentially firms had two sets of cashflows to meet: (i) investment in their operations to promote growth; and (ii) the payment of dividends. Without hedging, companies might be forced to under-invest because it would be costly or impossible to raise new finance and managers might not wish to cut dividends that would be viewed as a bad signal by the capital market (Lintner, 1956; Lonie et al. 1996).

All these above suggestions have been made to explain why companies use derivative products to hedge financial risk. The practical reasons of the particular hedging carried out by organisations to manage interest rate risk is now examined in the next section.

Risk management in practice: The case of interest rate risk[2]

There are a number of ways in which changes in interest rates can affect a business (Phillips, 1995). First, a company may have debt or bank loans linked to market interest rates, such as the bank base rate or LIBOR, and as interest rates change, the interest payable on these borrowings may also vary. The main focus of interest rate risk management is therefore to decide how much fixed and floating rate debt to have in the capital structure. A highly geared company, with a large amount of floating-rate debt financing in its capital structure, may suffer financial distress if interest rates increase dramatically, as shown by Example 8.4.

---

[2] This section of the chapter is based on Helliar et al. (2005).

Example 8.4

Assume a company has profit before interest and tax of GBP 100 million and has GBP 1 billion of debt in its capital structure. If interest rates are 5 per cent the interest charge would be GBP 50 million and profit after interest would be GBP 50 million. However, if interest rates rose to 10 per cent the interest charge would be GBP 100 million and the profit after interest would be zero. If the company had fixed-rate finance paying 6 per cent interest the profit after interest will be GBP 40 million irrespective of interest rate changes. Thus, interest rate risk is hedged by using fixed-rate funding in the capital structure.

A second reason why companies may experience interest rate risk is that they face the possibility that interest rates may fall reducing the interest income for an organisation that has surplus cash invested in monetary deposits and floating-rate investments. Third, an increase in interest rates may adversely affect a business if customers are reluctant to make purchases when interest rates are high because they have less disposable income available; this scenario is especially true for the UK where a high percentage of the population have mortgages with repayments linked to the bank base rate. Fourth, suppliers may suffer an increase in their funding costs when interest rates rise and wish to pass on the extra costs to their customers. This price increase may have a detrimental effect on the financial performance of the supplied business if it is not possible to pass on any raw material price increases to customers, especially where competition is fierce or the industry is regulated. For example, in a recession, a supermarket may be able to pass on price increases but a utility with an approved pricing policy, or a manufacturer of luxury goods, may not be able to do so. In the worst case scenario, high interest rates may increase both input costs and interest payments on finance, as well as encourage customers to postpone their purchases. Some organisations will be more exposed to the negative effects of high interest rates than others. Highly geared manufacturers of luxury goods are likely to be more sensitive to interest rate rises than low-geared supermarkets; the former will thus have far more to gain from managing their interest rate risk effectively.

The last few decades have seen an increase in the globalisation of the world's financial markets, and this may have affected the nature of interest rate risk management within companies. For example, Titman (2002) argues that practitioners often talk about 'windows of opportunity' and 'market conditions' when deciding upon fund raising and related hedging and cost reduction strategies. For example, the spread between AAA (highly rated with little chance of default) and BBB (lowest investment grade – more chance of default) rated debt has averaged about 120 basis points, but this spread changes substantially, both narrowing and widening at certain times in the economic cycle, as shown in Example 8.5.

Example 8.5

When the spread is wide, it is relatively more expensive for lower credit rated firms to raise finance. For example, if LIBOR was 5 per cent and the spread for AAA debt was 25 basis points, the AAA debt would have to pay a rate of 5.25 per cent. If the spread between AAA and BBB was 30 basis points the BBB debt would pay interest of 5.55 per cent. However, if the spread widened to 60 basis points between the AAA and BBB then the BBB would pay 5.85 per cent.

Companies are also likely to borrow in the shorter-term markets when the term structure of interest rates is positive and steep, but to borrow in the long-term debt markets when the yield curve is flatter or negative. Treasurers may adopt interest rate risk management techniques to reduce their cost of capital by timing the debt markets, as noted in Example 8.6.

Example 8.6

Assume interest rates are as follows:

Positive yield curve A		Flat yield curve B		Negative yield curve C	
Years to maturity	Interest rate %	Years to maturity	Interest rate %	Years to maturity	Interest rate %
1	4.00	1	4.00	1	6.50
3	4.50	3	4.00	3	5.75
5	5.00	5	4.00	5	5.00
10	5.75	10	4.00	10	4.50
20	6.50	20	4.00	20	4.00

The graphs of each of these would look very different as follows:

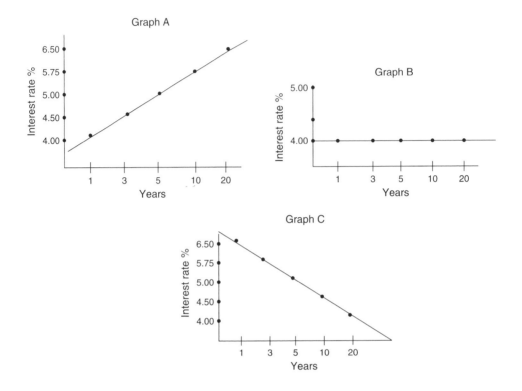

If interest rates were as in Graph A, companies would wish to issue short-term debt and pay interest of only 4 per cent over 1 year, or 4.5 per cent over 3 years. Companies would not wish to issue 20-year debt paying 6.50 per cent interest. In Graph B companies would be more likely to issue longer-term debt. If treasurers assumed that rates were going to rise in the future they would probably issue longer-term debt and possibly lock themselves into a rate of say 4 per cent over 10 years. If they expected interest rates to become lower, they would be more likely to issue shorter-term debt. In Graph C companies may well wish to lock into a low rate of interest over a 10- or 20-year horizon. Thus, the interest rate environment and expectations of interest rates will pay a large part in determining the maturity profile of the debt that is issued.

As noted above, a key feature of interest rate risk management is to decide on the proportion of fixed to floating rate debt. Ross (2002) describes treasurers' decisions on the fixed and floating rate debt mix, and advises on a two-stage methodology to deal with interest rate risk exposure. First, he suggests that an appropriate level of gearing is adopted, and second, for that level of gearing, an appropriate amount of fixed rate debt is selected. The maturity of the debt profile and gearing will be influenced by the desired credit rating and the stability of the businesses' cash flows. Where cash flows are volatile, a lower level of gearing is necessary. The more difficult decision, according to Ross, is the amount of debt to hedge, by fixing the interest payments and the maturity of this debt. This decision is affected by: (i) how the business responds to economic cycles; (ii) the effect that interest rate changes have on the company; (iii) the existence of banking covenants; and (iv) the competitive position of the organisation.

Douche (2002) suggests that companies should borrow floating rate finance if they expect rates to fall further than the yield curve suggests, or to borrow fixed rate finance otherwise, and to use options if they are uncertain. Most companies, however, are more likely to fix the interest rates on their funding in the short term, but this fixing tapers away to more floating-rate finance as the time horizon extends into the future. Highly geared companies, close to covenant restrictions, are likely to have more fixed rate finance in their debt structure as floating rate finance in the capital structure results in greater earnings volatility.

Companies that can change their prices as inflation rates rise can have mainly floating rate debt financing. In contrast, companies that cannot easily change their selling prices, have long-term contracts or anticipate fixed income cash flows, should lock in a margin by fixing their interest cost. The building and construction industry is a prime example of an industry where companies would probably wish to have fixed rate debt in their capital structure because of the long-term nature of their contracts. Indeed, Helliar et al. (2005) find that companies usually set a policy on the limits of how much of their debt should be at fixed rates – usually between 25 and 75 per cent. Thus treasurers have a wide amount of discretion about how much of their firms' debt to keep at fixed rates and how much at floating rates of interest. This percentage changes as the interest rate environment changes, and treasurers use interest rate swaps to manage this debt profile. Helliar et al. (2005) also found in their interviews and survey of interest rate risk management that most companies had a formal Financial Risk Management Policy document. This generally detailed the amount of funding that should be fixed, with ranges set both by currency and for different periods out into the future. However, smaller companies were less likely to have formalised their interest rate risk management policy to the same extent as larger company counterparts.

Covenants are a major factor in interest rate risk management and Ross (2002) advises that companies need to manage their debt to earnings before interest, tax, depreciation and amortisation (EBITDA) ratio or their EBITDA to interest expense ratio. This is both from a practical point of view and also from a self-preservation perspective as these ratios are often included in covenant agreements. For example, Mortimer (2003) notes that 'the volatility of interest rate payments can affect the credit rating and covenant interest coverage ratios' (p. 47).

The sector that an organisation is in also affects the interest rate risk management decisions that are taken. Douche (2002) states that building and construction companies should hold fixed rate finance as demand for their products normally goes down as interest rates go up. This preference for fixed-rate funding can be achieved by issuing fixed rate debt or by using interest-rate swaps to change the debt profile from floating to fixed rate finance. However, Douche suggests that retail organisations should buy caps (options) to put a ceiling on the amount of interest that they may have to pay, as the retail industry is very competitive, and the cost of borrowing is often a crucial component of firm profitability in this sector. However, as caps are costly derivative products, he recommends that retailers should use floating rate finance and only use caps when they really believe interest rates will rise. For general businesses, he recommends that treasurers take a view about the future and, if they think that rates are going down, they should take out the maximum amount of floating rate finance possible, but if they expect rates to increase, they should have the highest amount possible of fixed rate finance. Thus, Douche expects treasurers to take an active view on the movement of interest rates and to base their hedging decisions on these views.

The gearing of a company and the mix of fixed to floating rate debt is a key issue, but other factors that affect interest rate risk management is the type of debt, maturity and currency of issue. Helliar et al. (2005) find that UK companies often raise funding through banks with only about a quarter of non-equity financing being raised via the issue of bonds. The term, or time frame, of the debt raised is generally medium term, from about 4 to 7 years. Most funds are raised in either sterling or US dollars, indicating that the US is of major importance to UK firms. Raising finance in Euros is not so popular, and may reflect hostility to the Euro within the UK or, alternatively, the fact that the UK is not in the Euro zone. However, companies with operations overseas are more likely to raise finance in the foreign currencies of the countries where their operations are located.

When determining their interest rate policy, UK companies appear to review the direction of interest rates and the magnitude of interest rate changes, but are ambivalent about Gross Domestic Product (GDP) which reflects general business conditions, and industry trends. Inflation and deflationary indicators are also important, but not to the same extent as interest rates. A variety of external forecasts are used to help inform these views, including those offered by banks, economists, analysts as well as information service providers such as Bloomberg and Reuters. Many UK companies base their interest rate risk management policy upon the shape of the current yield curve, projections of interest rates changes in the future, and the spreads between different credit ratings.

Risk management practices increase as the size of the organisation rises since interest rate risk is of more concern to larger companies than to their smaller-sized counterparts. Smaller companies possibly have more pressing needs such as strategy implementation, establishing a loyal customer base and sourcing raw materials rather than fine-tuning the management of financial risk.

The Helliar et al. (2005) study shows that there are three factors that appear to be important in explaining why companies attempt to manage their interest rate risk: (i) the need to manage reported profits; (ii) the desire to protect share-holder funds; and (iii) where the interest charge to EBIT/EBITDA is significant. Surprisingly, factors such as a high dividend payout ratio or poor financial ratios do not appear to impact on UK companies' interest rate risk management decisions.

Summary

This chapter has highlighted the financial risks that companies face: interest rate risk; foreign exchange rate risk; commodity price risk; and equity price risk. The chapter summarises the four classes of derivative products that can be used to hedge financial risk, swaps, options, futures and forward, with particular emphasis on interest rate and exchange rate products. The chapter then examines the reasons why companies may want to adopt financial risk management practices and documents interest rate risk management in practice. Overall, financial risk management is of vital importance to companies. This can be demonstrated by the enormous growth of the derivatives markets over the last couple of decades that allow financial managers to hedge their financial risks in practice.

References

Belk, P. and Glaum, M. (1990). 'The Management of Foreign Exchange Risk in UK Multinationals: An Empirical Investigation', *Accounting and Business Research*, Vol. 21, No. 81, pp. 3–13.

Douche, N. (2002). 'Applying the Best Strategy', *The Treasurer*, June, pp. 51–52.

Eckl, S. and Robinson, J.N. (1990). 'Some Issues in Corporate Hedging Policy', *Accounting and Business Research*, Vol. 20, No. 80, pp. 287–298.

Froot, K.A., Scharfstein, D.S. and Stein, J.C. (1993). 'Risk Management: Coordinating Corporate Investment and Financing Policies', *Journal of Finance*, Vol. XLVIII, No. 5, pp. 1629–1658.

Froot, K.A., Scharfstein, D.S. and Stein, J.C. (1994). 'A Framework for Risk Management', *Harvard Business Review*, Vol. 72, Nov./Dec., pp. 91–102.

Gilson, S.C. (1989). 'Management Turnover and Financial Distress', *Journal of Financial Economics*, Vol. 25, pp. 241–262.

Helliar, C.V. (1997). *Uses of Interest Rate and Currency Swaps by Financial Managers*. CIMA Monograph, London.

Helliar, C.V., Dhanani, A., Fifield, S. and Stevenson, L. (2005). *Interest Rate Risk Management*. CIMA Publishing, Oxford.

Holland, J.B. (1993). *International Financial Management*, 2nd edn. Blackwell, Oxford.

Lintner, J. (1956). 'Distribution of Incomes of Corporations among Dividends, Retained Earnings, and Taxes', *American Economic Review*, Vol. 46, No. 2, pp. 97–113.

Lonie, A.A., Abeyratna, G., Power, D.M. and Sinclair, C.D. (1996). 'The Stock Market Reaction Dividend Announcements: A UK Study of Complex Market Signals', *Journal of Economic Studies*, 23 (1), pp. 32–52.

Mian, S.L. (1996). 'Evidence on Corporate Hedging Policy', *Journal of Financial and Quantitative Analysis*, Vol. 31, No. 3, pp. 419–439.

Modigliani, F. and Miller, M.H. (1958). 'The Cost of Capital, Corporation Finance and the Theory of Investment', *American Economic Review*, Vol. XLVIII, pp. 261–297.

Mortimer, S. (2003). 'Gaining the Right Exposure', *The Treasurer*, May, pp. 46–48.

Nance, D.R., Smith, C.W. and Smithson, C.W. (1993). 'On the Determinants of Corporate Hedging', *Journal of Finance*, Vol. 48, pp. 267–284.

Phillips, A. (1995). '1995 Derivatives Practices and Instruments Survey', *Financial Management*, Vol. 24, No. 2, Summer, pp. 115–125.

Rawls, S.W. and Smithson, C.W. (1990). 'Strategic Risk Management', *Continental Bank Journal of Applied Corporate Finance*, Vol. 1, pp. 59–72.

Ross, D. (2002). 'No Perfect Answer', *Accountancy*, Aug, pp. 87.

Sercu, P. and Uppal, R. (1995). *International Financial Markets and the Firm*. South West College Publishing, Ohio.

Smith, C.W. and Stultz, R. (1985). 'The Determinants of Firms' Hedging Policies', *Journal of Financial and Quantitative Analysis*, Vol. 20, pp. 391–405.

Stultz, R.M. (1984). 'Optimal Hedging Policies', *Journal of Financial and Quantitative Analysis*, Vol. 19, pp. 127–140.

Stultz, R.M. (1996). 'Rethinking Risk Management', *Journal of Applied Corporate Finance*, Vol. 9, No. 3, pp. 8–24.

Titman, S. (2002). 'The Modigliani and Miller Theorem and the Integration of Financial Markets', *Financial Management*, Spring, pp. 101–115.

Tufano, P. (1998). 'Agency Costs of Corporate Risk Management', *Financial Management*, Spring, pp. 67–77.

Risk Reporting: Development, Regulation and Current Practice

Philip Linsley[*], Philip Shrives[†] and Peter Kajüter[‡]

[*]*University of York, UK*
[†]*Northumbria University, UK*
[‡]*University of Münster, Germany*

Introduction

Shareholders are aware that any investment they hold in a company is subject to risk. Media coverage of company failures, falls in stock market indices and other adverse company news bulletins remind the investment community that this is the case. The outcome is that even when investors act irrationally (and it is their prerogative to act as they wish) they still have an underlying appreciation that share prices are volatile and this can result in losses as well as gains in their portfolios. High profile events receive extensive amounts of press and television coverage and, consequently, they act as particularly strong reminders that risk is fundamental to stock market investment. For example, a spate of prominent accounting scandals at Enron, WorldCom, Parmalat, and other companies became topics of great interest when they first occurred and have continued to remain newsworthy. Cases such as Enron may therefore be one reason why shareholders' awareness of risk appears to have increased in recent years.

Also companies have become more attentive to risk latterly. In part this may be caused by having to operate in more aggressive business environments where change is continuous. It may also, in part, be a result of directors becoming conscious of shareholders' increased concerns about risk. This rise in interest in risk has been accompanied by a rise in interest in risk management and these are, of course, related. Directors are looking to reduce and manage company risk exposures as this creates a more stable company and this then allays the anxieties of shareholders.

If directors are developing a better understanding of the risks their company faces and are improving risk management in the company then this should be reassuring for shareholders. However, it will only be reassuring if the shareholders are made aware of the risk management actions the directors have undertaken; therefore, this risk and risk management information has to be communicated to the outside world if it is to be useful. If there is a lack of transparency in the disclosure of risk information, then shareholders cannot ensure their portfolios fully take into account the risk profiles of the companies they have invested into.

As shareholders bear the risk of investing it seems only reasonable that they receive proper information that will assist their management of this risk. Consequently, there have been calls for companies to provide greater amounts of risk information within their annual reports as this is considered one of the principal disclosure vehicles. For example, the risk disclosure debate in the UK can be traced back to 1998 when the Institute of Chartered Accountants in England and Wales (ICAEW) published a discussion paper 'Financial Reporting of Risk – Proposals for a Statement of Business Risk' (ICAEW, 1998). In the same year, a mandatory risk reporting requirement in the statutory management report was introduced in Germany and accompanied by an Accounting Principle of the German Institute of Chartered Accountants (IDW, 1998).

The premise upon which the ICAEW's 1998 paper was built was that the risk information and risk management information contained within annual reports was ad hoc, and consequently only partial risk information was being made available to the marketplace. Such risk information that was being disclosed often resulted from the mandatory disclosure requirements of certain accounting standards that only addressed very specific areas of risk (for example, in relation to financial instruments). The ICAEW acknowledged that at that time it was recommended listed UK companies disclose risks within the Operating and Financial Review section of the annual report, but companies were able to interpret this recommendation as they saw fit. Anecdotally, the belief was that in fact very little risk information was being provided and hence there was a lack of transparency in respect of risk information. Therefore, the principal proposal of the discussion paper was that directors should be reporting upon risks and the management of those risks in a coherent manner such that shareholders and other readers of the annual report can understand the *full* risk picture for that particular company.

In this chapter we examine the risk reporting debate by initially considering the development of the debate. We then review and compare risk reporting regulation across a range of different countries. When the ICAEW produced the 1998 discussion paper and mandatory risk reporting was introduced in Germany, there had been no risk research performed; this is no longer the case and a summary of the findings of current research is presented. Examples of current risk disclosures are then discussed before conclusions are drawn.

Developing ideas of risk reporting: A call for volunteers

The ICAEW have not been alone in proposing that risk reporting should be improved. The 1997 American Accounting Association/Financial Accounting Standards Board (AAA/FASB) conference debated the subject of risk disclosure as they, like the ICAEW, had perceived that companies were providing insufficient risk information (Schrand and Elliott, 1998).

Professional bodies in other countries have also considered the issue of risk disclosure important and issued related discussion papers and risk reporting guidelines (see Table 9.1 for summary).

Table 9.1 Examples of professional body discussion papers and guidelines

Professional body	Papers or guidelines published	Summary of paper or guideline
Institute of Chartered Accountants in England and Wales (ICAEW)	Financial reporting of risk – Proposals for a Statement of Business Risk (1998) No Surprises: The Case for Better Risk Reporting (1999) No Surprises: Working for Better Risk Reporting (2002)	Related discussion papers proposing that directors should report upon risks and the management of those risks in a coherent manner such that the *full* risk picture for that company can be understood. The suggestion was directors should voluntarily prepare a statement of business risk for inclusion within the annual report. The benefits of disclosing risk information are also discussed
The Canadian Institute of Chartered Accountants (CICA)	Management's Discussion and Analysis – Guidance on Preparation and Disclosure (2002; amended 2004) Risk Disclosures MD&A Interpretive Release (2006)	CICA guidance issued through the Canadian Performance Reporting Board (CPRB) on the preparation of the MD&A. Section 360 provides specific guidance to directors on the reporting of risks, recommending that companies disclose significant risks together with information on how those risks are managed. Updated in 2004 to reflect the greater risk disclosure requirements in the Annual Information Form (see Table 9.2). CICA Risk Disclosures MD&A Interpretive Release provides guidance on what types of risks should be disclosed, how they should be disclosed and where they should be located in the MD&A

(continued)

Table 9.1 (*Continued*)

Professional body	Papers or guidelines published	Summary of paper or guideline
Fédération des Experts Comptables Européens (FEE)	Risk Management and Internal Control in the EU – Discussion Paper (2005)	Discussion paper intended to improve risk management and internal control in European companies following corporate governance failures in companies such as Parmalat and Enron. FEE recognises that related to the topic of risk management is the issue of the disclosure of specific risks and hence the paper incorporates relevant risk disclosure discussions
International Accounting Standards Board (IASB)	Management Commentary – Discussion Paper (2005)	The MD&A to be an essential component of the financial report and the inclusion of a discussion of risks and uncertainties is seen as indispensable to the MD&A if it is to fulfil its objective of assisting investors to interpret the financial statements and understand the critical issues facing the company. Detailed discussion, and examples, of good and bad risk reporting practice are included in the paper
Accounting Standards Board (ASB)	Reporting Statement: Operating and Financial Review (2006)	The reporting statement sets out (non-mandatory) good practice in the preparation of the OFR or MD&A. This replaces previous guidance following changes in UK company law. A discussion of principal risks and uncertainties is considered integral to the OFR as is information on how the directors manage these risks and uncertainties. Implementation guidance is provided with examples of disclosures

(*continued*)

Table 9.1 (*Continued*)

Professional body	Papers or guidelines published	Summary of paper or guideline
American Institute of Certified Public Accountants/ Certified Management Accountants Canada (AICPA/CMA Canada)	Guideline on the Reporting of Organizational Risks for Internal and External Decision Making (2006)	Detailed guidance on how to report on risk both for internal and external purposes through an integrated *Risk Reporting Model*. The guideline discusses why risk reporting is important and how it adds to shareholder value through aiding in the strategic decision management of the company. Voluntary disclosure of risk information is argued for and the benefits of doing so are discussed

The professional body discussion papers habitually note that the annual report needs to comprise more than the financial statements – the balance sheet, profit and loss account, cash-flow statement and notes to the accounts. A narrative report prepared by the directors is needed to supplement and discuss the financial statements. The name that is attached to this narrative discussion may differ (for example, it is variously referred to as the 'Operating and Financial Review' (OFR), 'Management's Discussion and Analysis' (MD&A or MDA), the 'Management Report', the 'Management Commentary' (MC) and the 'Business Review') but it is considered essential for interpreting the financial results of the company.

For example, The Canadian Institute of Chartered Accountants (CICA) 2002 publication 'Guidance on the Preparation and Disclosure of the MD&A' states that the purpose of the MD&A is to 'give a reader the ability to look at the issuer thorough the eyes of management' (p. 13) and should therefore contain five essential elements:

1. The company's vision, core businesses and strategy
2. Key performance drivers
3. Capabilities to achieve desired results
4. An analysis of historical and prospective results
5. The risks that may shape and effect the achievement of results.

The fifth element addresses the issue of risk reporting and recommends disclosure of key risks and uncertainties, risk management procedures and strategies, and discussions of the potential impacts of risks upon results. CICA's updated MD&A guidance (2004) and Interpretive Release (2006) reflect increased risk disclosure requirements in Canada and hence give even more prominence to risk reporting.

Internationally, the IASB (International Accounting Standards Board) has published a 'Management Commentary – Discussion Paper' (2005) that affirms the importance of providing risk information. This extensive paper states:

> The MC should set out and discuss the key resources, risks and relationships, relating to the entity, that will assist in the pursuit of its objectives. . . . Reporting on the key risks and uncertainties facing an entity, together with a commentary on managements' approach to them, is a critical aspect of MC. Risks might arise from the external environment, dependencies on others or the management of resources, both financial and non-financial. The risks facing an entity will reflect its particular circumstances. (pp. 40–41)

Transparency of risk information has not just been seen as a matter for accounting-related bodies to be concerned about. Significant international non-accounting organisations have also contributed to this debate with IOSCO (International Organization of Securities Commissions), OECD (Organisation for Economic Co-operation and Development) and UNCTAD (United Nations Conference on Trade and Development), all publishing disclosure-related documents that underscore the need for risk information to be placed in the public domain. Figure 9.1 provides extracts of their disclosure principles.

International Organization of Securities Commissions (IOSCO)	United Nations Conference on Trade and Development (UNCTAD)	Organisation for Economic Co-operation and Development (OECD)
General Principles Regarding Disclosure of Management's Discussion and Analysis of Financial Condition and Results of Operations (2003)	*Guidance in Good Practices on Corporate Governance Disclosure (2006)*	*OECD Principles of Corporate Governance (2004)*
'disclose the potential impact of currently known trends, events and uncertainties that are reasonably likely to have material effects on a company's financial condition or results of operations ... and ... provide information about the risks to a company's earnings and cash flow'.	'to assist developing countries and countries with economies in transition to improve their enterprises' accountability ... users of financial information and participants in the marketplace need information on foreseeable material risks'.	'disclosure should include ... material information on ... foreseeable risk factors ... disclosure of risk is most effective when it is tailored to the particular industry in question ... disclosure about the system for monitoring and managing risk is increasingly regarded as good practice'.

Figure 9.1 Extracts from IOSCO UNCTAD and IOSCO disclosure principles

One feature of the discussion papers issued by professional bodies such as CICA, the ICAEW and the American Institute of Certified Public Accountants/Certified Management Accountants Canada (AICPA/CMA Canada) is that they recommended directors should provide risk disclosures on a *voluntary* basis. They were not proposing mandatory disclosure requirements. If directors are to be persuaded that it is worthwhile to voluntarily disclose risk information, then the benefits of doing so must be attractive.

One benefit of providing transparent risk information in the annual report is that it ensures that all categories of shareholders receive identical risk information. Thus, as a public document, the annual report is a means of ensuring there is parity of treatment for all shareholders whether they are a large institutional investor or a small private investor. Consequently no shareholder group is privileged. Further, when directors commence disclosing risk information then this can act as a stimulus for them to improve their risk management abilities. That is, as external stakeholders will be able to scrutinise how risks and uncertainties have been handled within the company, then the directors will have an incentive to report year-on-year how the risk management system and processes have evolved and to explain the impact this has had on the company's risk profile.

From the director's stance, a more significant benefit that is frequently cited is the impact that risk disclosure may have upon the cost of capital (Courtnage, 1998). The argument put forward is that if lenders of finance are better informed about the risks a company is subject to and how the directors manage those risks, then this will result in a reduction in the cost of finance. The reduction in the cost of finance arises because the lenders now have an increased confidence in the company and its management, and can therefore remove the interest rate premium that has been incorporated to cover for uncertainty on the part of the lender. Ultimately, if there is a reduction in the cost of finance then this will be of direct financial benefit to the company. The other principal benefit relates to the discussions within the professional body reports as to the orientation of the MD&A narrative. There is strong support for the MD&A discussions, including the risk-related discussions, to be forward-looking (Courtnage, 1998; Linsley and Shrives, 2000). Whilst the results in the financial statements are historical and backward-looking, it is considered important that investors can make assessments as to whether the reported results are representative of the future and can also appreciate the important factors that may affect future results. Therefore it is beneficial to investors if forward-looking risk information is disclosed, as this is of greater practical use in determining whether the shares in a particular company should remain in their portfolios or be sold.

Risk reporting regulation

The professional bodies' requests in the early 2000s for directors to voluntarily disclose risk information were relatively unsuccessful. The directors weighed the benefits against the potential costs of disclosure and found the scales tipped in favour of non-disclosure. The principal benefit for directors is a potential lowering of the cost of capital. There is some empirical support from academic studies for stating that increased disclosure *generally* leads to a reduced cost of capital (Botosan, 1997; Hail, 2002), but this may not be well known within the business community, and there have been no studies that have specifically linked increased risk disclosures to a reduced cost of capital. Consequently, the benefits may have appeared rather lightweight to directors.

Potential costs were, however, viewed as substantial with two primary concerns being raised. First, there was a difficulty with the provision of forward-looking risk information. It is relatively easy to discuss a risk that has already occurred, but it is much more difficult to discuss a future risk. (Just as it is easy to say that it rained heavily yesterday, but it is much more difficult to say if it will rain in 3 months' time and whether it will be a light shower or a downpour and what the impact will be.) The nature of risks is that they do not always crystallise and when they do it may be in an unexpected form. Directors were particularly concerned that they may become liable to investors who had acted upon future risk information that was subsequently found to be inaccurate. Exposure to litigation based on the disclosure of forward-looking information is, as one would expect, of most concern in countries where safe-harbour protection is not in place.

The second major concern was that some risk information may be commercially sensitive and releasing it into the public domain would put a company at a competitive disadvantage. These so-called 'proprietary' costs of disclosure may be substantial for some companies. For example, discussions about how a company is managing the risk of competitors taking away market share could be very valuable information for any of those competitor companies. Suggesting that companies be permitted exemption from disclosing any commercially sensitive risk information is not particularly helpful. Investors attempting to judge the risk position of a company would then not know if they were viewing a full or partial picture of the company. Additionally, some companies can take advantage of such an exemption by claiming all their risk information is commercially sensitive. Companies claiming such an exemption can then produce 'boilerplate' risk disclosures that contain little company-specific risk information, with the end result being that the company says little more than that it is managing its risk. The latter may reassure investors to some small degree, but beyond that it is not useful information. It is not surprising therefore that the voluntary approach was usurped by a mandatory approach to risk reporting.

This was the approach taken in Germany in response to prominent corporate failures and bankruptcies with the Corporate Control and Transparency Act (KonTraG) introducing the requirement to report on material risks in the management report in 1998 (§§ 289 and 315 German Commercial Code (Handelsgesetzbuch – HGB)). This legislation took effect in 1999 and concerned all medium and large public limited companies. Since the law did not provide any guidance on risk reporting, the German Institute of Chartered Accountants (IDW) defined some rules for risk disclosures (IDW, 1998). To further specify the legal reporting requirements, the German Accounting Standards Board (GASB) issued a specific German Accounting Standard on risk reporting (GAS 5) that became effective in 2001. In line with the law, GAS 5 focuses on the downside risk and specifies both content and format of such risk disclosures. For example, individual risks and their possible consequences shall be described, a risk which threatens the existence of the enterprise shall be clearly presented as such. Moreover, risks shall be classified into risk categories and the risk report shall be presented in a separate section of the management report.

Given the experience in Germany, the GASB suggested to the EU to introduce a mandatory risk reporting as part of the annual report in all EU member states. The EU followed this idea in the 2003 Accounts Modernization Directive (2003/51/EC) and the 2004 Transparency Directive (2004/109/EC). European Union member states are obliged to implement these directives which require the annual report to incorporate a management report which includes a 'description of the principal risks and uncertainties', and requires the interim management report to describe 'the principal risks and uncertainties for the remaining six months of the financial year'. Consequently, in Germany the 2004 Reform Act on Accounting (Bilanzrechtsreformgesetz – BilReG) was introduced to enact the EU directives by amending the German Commercial Code (Handelsgesetzbuch – HGB) so that not only risks but also opportunities have had to be reported since 2005. Moreover, the French Commercial Code (Code de Commerce) was amended by Order No. 2004-1832 to reflect the EU requirements in France, and in the UK the Companies Act 2006 will require risks and uncertainties to be described within the Business Review section of the annual report once it comes into effect. The result of the EU directives has been to initiate changes in company law provisions in member states and this has brought about some convergence in risk reporting practice in the EU.

In the USA and Canada the risk reporting requirements show similarities to one another. Annual forms have to be filed in both countries and as part of the filing there must be disclosure of 'risk factors'. It is also necessary to file an MDA that discusses risks, uncertainties, challenges and opportunities. A difference between these North American and European regulations is in the location of the risk disclosures. The North American risk disclosures are sited within the annual forms filed with The Securities Exchange Commission (SEC) in the USA or The Canadian Securities Administrators (CSA) in Canada. Therefore the USA and Canadian risk disclosures *may* also form a part of the annual report but do not have to; whereas the European risk disclosures are included within the annual report. Table 9.2 provides a summary of risk reporting regulations in a range of countries.

Table 9.2 Summary of risk reporting regulations in selected countries

Country	Summary of risk reporting regulations
USA	The Securities Exchange Act of 1934 requires US companies to file Form 10-K annually and Item 1A requires disclosure of risk factors. US companies also have to file Form 10-Q on a quarterly basis and this requires disclosure of any material changes to risk factors disclosed in Form 10-K.
	Non-US companies are required to file Form 20-F annually and this also requires disclosure of risk factors. 'Companies are encouraged to list the risk factors in the order of their priority. Risk factors may include, for example: the nature of the business in which it is engaged or proposes to engage; factors relating to the countries in which it operates; the absence of profitable operations in recent periods; . . . reliance on the expertise of management; potential dilution; unusual competitive conditions; pending expiration of material patents, trademarks or contracts; or dependence on a limited number of customers or suppliers.'
	Forms 10-K and 20-F also require the preparation of an MD&A. The SEC has provided guidance on the MD&A under Financial Reporting Release (FRR) 72 'Interpretation: Commission Guidance Regarding Management's

(*continued*)

Table 9.2 (*Continued*)

Country	Summary of risk reporting regulations
	Discussion and Analysis of Financial Condition and Results of Operations'. The guidance states the MD&A should 'identify and disclose known trends, events, demands, commitments and uncertainties that are reasonably likely to have a material effect on financial condition or operating performance' and 'provide insight into material opportunities, challenges and risks, such as those presented by known material trends and uncertainties, on which the company's executives are most focused for both the short and long term, as well as the actions they are taking to address these opportunities, challenges and risks'.
Canada	The Canadian Securities Administrators (CSA) National Instrument 51-102 Continuous Disclosure Obligations requires Canadian companies to file MD&As that 'discuss important trends and risks that have affected the financial statements, and trends and risks that are reasonably likely to affect them in the future'. The company's overall performance must be discussed and this includes 'an analysis of . . . known trends, demands, commitments, events or uncertainties that are reasonably likely to have an effect on your company's business'. The results of operations must 'discuss your analysis of your company's operations . . . including: commitments, events, risks or uncertainties that you reasonably believe will materially affect your company's future performance'.
	An annual information form (AIF) has to be filed that 'describes your company, its operations and prospects, risks and other external factors that impact your company specifically.' A section on risk factors must be included in the AIF. This requires companies to 'disclose risk factors relating to your company and its business, such as . . . experience of management, the general risks inherent in the business carried on by your company, environmental and health risks, reliance on key personnel, regulatory constraints, economic or political conditions and financial history and any other matter that would be most likely to influence an investor's decision to purchase securities of your company. Risks should be disclosed in the order of their seriousness'.
France	Article 222-3 of the General Regulation of the Autorité des Marchés Financiers (AMF) requires the annual report to contain a management report that includes 'a description of the principal risks and uncertainties that (the company) face(s)'. Under article 222-6 the half-yearly interim

(*continued*)

Table 9.2 (Continued)

Country	Summary of risk reporting regulations
	management report must 'describe the principal risks and uncertainties for the remaining six months of the year'. These regulations are a part of French company law and hence included within the French Commercial Code (Code de Commerce).
Germany	The German Commercial Code (Handelsgesetzbuch – HGB) requires medium and large public limited companies to prepare a management report. The Corporate Control and Transparency Act introduced a mandatory risk disclosure requirement in 1998. Subsequently, the Reform Act on Accounting (Bilanzrechtsreformgesetz – BilReG) amended previous reporting requirements in the HGB in 2004 and companies are now required to describe material risks and opportunities.
	In 2000, the German Accounting Standards Board (GASB) has issued a detailed accounting standard GAS 5 specifying how risks shall be reported under the provisions of the HGB. This comprises a generic standard 'Risk Reporting' and two industry-specific standards relating to financial service institutions and to insurance companies. The standard focuses on providing users with relevant and reliable information for decision-making, which would allow users to form an understanding of risks affecting future developments. GAS 5 requires a risk report to be prepared as a separate section in the management report. The Risk Reporting standard provides an example of possible ways of categorising risks, and requires that risks should be quantified if possible, provided that models and assumptions are described. Interdependencies between risks need to be articulated.
UK	The Companies Act 2006 (coming into force in 2008) states that a director's report must be included within the annual report and this must contain a business review (§ 415). The business review must include a 'description of principal risks and uncertainties facing the company' (§ 417(3)(a)).
Australia	In 2006, The Australian Stock Exchange (ASX) Corporate Governance Council issued a consultation document on the Principles of Good Corporate Governance & Best Practice Recommendations. Guidance provided in relation to the interpretation of Principle 7 'Recognise and Manage Risk' recommends that it is good practice that companies include a description of their risk profile within their annual report. These are currently proposals and should come into effect after July 2007.

The annual report is normally considered the prime corporate disclosure document and consequently some commentators believe this is where the most significant disclosures should be located. The annual filings to the SEC and CSA are, however, public documents just as much as the annual report. Therefore, as long as company information is made relatively easy to access, it seems reasonable to expect investors to access an annual filing.

Current risk disclosure practice

Earlier in the chapter it has been remarked that the ICAEW and FASB/AAA had called for greater risk disclosure based on the belief that current company risk reporting was inadequate. In the late 1990s and early 2000s professional bodies, regulators and other interested parties had no research data or surveys to draw upon to confirm this belief and evidence used tended to be anecdotal. Subsequently risk disclosure studies have been carried out that provide a more objective basis for discussions. The academic studies summarised in Table 9.3 have examined annual report risk disclosures for German, Italian, UK and Canadian companies, and UK and Canadian banks.

Some of the principal findings of these studies are: it is unusual to quantify the size of a risk or to place a monetary value upon the risk, there is greater disclosure of past risks than future risks, and generally the risk disclosures are found to be somewhat vague.

Quantification of risk is important as it enhances the value of the risk disclosure. That is, knowing the size of a risk can inform the reader of its potential impact upon profitability, cash flows or capital. It is perhaps understandable that directors provide relatively little quantified risk information as it can be a very difficult task to assess the size of a risk. Additionally if, for example, the company is facing the risk of litigation, the directors could be reluctant to disclose an estimate of the company's risk exposure as this may be construed as an admission of guilt.

If there is less disclosure of future risks than past risks this confirms the views of some of the professional bodies that insufficient forward-looking information has been provided. This hampers the usefulness of the risk disclosures. The reasons why directors may be reluctant to discuss future risks have been discussed earlier in the chapter. It should be noted, however, that the most recent study by Linsley and Shrives (2006b) does not confirm this reluctance to disclose forward-looking risk information. Furthermore, a longitudinal study by

Table 9.3 Summary of risk disclosure research

Author(s)	Title of research	Focus of research	Principal findings
Kajüter (2001)	Risk disclosure: results of an empirical study and the Exposure Draft of GAS 5 (in German)	Examines annual report risk disclosures of 82 German companies	Limited risk information is disclosed and there is a lack of coherence in the disclosures
Woods and Reber (2003)	A comparison of UK and German reporting practice in respect of disclosure post GAS 5	Examines annual report risk disclosures of 6 German and 6 UK companies pre- and post-GAS 5 implementation	GAS 5 had a positive effect upon the quantity of risk disclosures in the annual reports of the German companies. Limited reporting of forward-looking risk information and of the size of the risks occurs
Beretta and Bozzolan (2004)	A Framework for the Analysis of Firm Risk Communication	Examines annual report risk disclosures of 85 Italian non-financial companies	Limited reporting of forward-looking risk information and in discussions of future risks there is a reluctance to indicate whether the impact will be positive or negative
Lajili and Zéghal (2005)	A Content Analysis of Risk Management Disclosures in Canadian Annual Reports	Examines annual report risk disclosures by Toronto Stock Exchange (TSE) 300 largest companies	Focus is on reporting upon financial risks, commodity risks and market risks. Emphasis on reporting negative aspects of risk rather than the opportunities it may present. Risks are discussed qualitatively and there is little quantification

Table 9.3 (Continued)

Author(s)	Title of research	Focus of research	Principal findings
Kajüter (2006)	Risk disclosures of listed firms in Germany: a longitudinal study	Examines annual report risk disclosures of 80 German-listed companies over a 5-year period (1999–2003)	Significant increase in risk disclosures over the 5-year period; risk reports remain nevertheless vague; firms report more external than internal risks; number of risk disclosures increases with firm size
Linsley and Shrives (2006a)	Risk Disclosure: An Exploratory Study of UK and Canadian Banks	Examines annual report risk disclosures of 9 UK and 9 Canadian banks	Limited reporting of forward-looking risk information and limited quantification of risks
Linsley and Shrives (2006b)	Risk Reporting: A Study of Risk Disclosures in the Annual Reports of UK Companies	Examines annual report risk disclosures of 79 UK non-financial companies	Companies appear willing to disclose forward-looking risks, and are more likely to disclose good risk news than bad risk news. There is no association between the company's general risk level and the number of risk disclosures

Kajüter (2006) shows a continuous increase in risk disclosures of German listed firms over a 5-year period from 1999 to 2003.

There is mixed evidence from the studies as to whether directors are more or less willing to discuss risk in its positive form (as opportunity) than in its negative form (as the possibility of bad things happening). For example, compare the results of Lajili and Zéghal (2005) with Linsley and Shrives (2006b). A potential preference of directors for disclosing positive risk news can be explained as follows. Positive risk news reflects well upon the directors as it can represent, for example, discussions about the successful exploitation of opportunities or explanations of how a risk has been successfully managed. Conversely, directors may be less willing to disclose bad risk news as this might reflect upon their reputation as managers. This does not imply that companies will withhold *all* bad risk news. Bad news may need to be disclosed if the financial results are such that, had the directors omitted an explanation for the results this would merely arouse suspicion and potentially damage their reputations to a greater extent than if the information had not been disclosed. The directors may also be more willing to disclose bad risk news if they can attribute this to external factors and therefore deflect blame away from their own management actions and abilities (Kajüter, 2006). Directors could also be prepared to release bad news into the public domain via the annual report if they want to pre-warn of possible difficulties in the future. Therefore there are a number of reasons why bad news will be disclosed.

These studies try to understand and interpret *overall* risk disclosure patterns. Individual companies will, however, exhibit different levels of risk disclosure as the extracts in Table 9.4 demonstrate. In Example 1 significant risks are

Table 9.4 Risk disclosure examples

Example 1	**Marine Produce Australia Limited – 2006 annual report extract**
	Major risks arise from such matters as actions by competitors, government policy changes, difficulties in sourcing raw materials, the robustness of the technologies being developed to commercially cultivate the prawns and fish, environment, occupational health and safety, financial reporting and the purchase, development and use of information systems (p. 6)
Example 2	**Carrs Milling Industries plc – 2006 annual report extract**
	Market conditions for Agriculture are not getting any easier with the low farm gate milk price and again unbelievable expected delays of the Single Farm Payment. The massive increase in wheat prices combined with high-energy costs will make it a tough year for the Food division. Engineering made good progress this period, but this is unlikely to be repeated in the current period.
	The markets in which all three businesses operate are competitive both in terms of pricing from other suppliers and the retail environment in general which has a direct impact on many of our customers. Despite this, Carr's businesses have a long record of increasing sales and profits through a combination of investing in modern efficient factories, developing a range of quality products and making sound acquisitions (pp. 9–10)

(*continued*)

Table 9.4 (*Continued*)

Example 3	**Hugo Boss AG – 2006 annual report extract**

Market risk and opportunities

As a fashion and lifestyle company, every new season confronts HUGO BOSS with the risk that portions of the new collections may be received by the market less positively than anticipated.

HUGO BOSS counters this risk by means of centralized creation of fashion collections and a globally consistent brand image. Constant market observation and regular attendance at international fashion fairs ensure that trends are identified early on to serve as a basis for the collections.

Risk is also mitigated by the multi-season concept along with the broad range of collections encompassing all HUGO BOSS brands and a market presence in over 100 countries with some 5700 points of sale (pp. 79–80)

Example 4	**The Coca-Cola Company – 2005 10-K risk factors extract**

Increase in cost, disruption of supply or shortage of raw materials could harm our business

We and our bottling partners use various raw materials in our business including high fructose corn syrup, sucrose, aspartame, saccharin, acesulfame potassium, sucralose and orange juice concentrate. The prices for these raw materials fluctuate depending on market conditions. Substantial increases in the prices for our raw materials, to the extent they cannot be recouped through increases in the prices of finished beverage products, would increase our and the Coca-Cola system's operating costs and could reduce our profitability. Increases in the prices of our finished products resulting from higher raw material costs could affect affordability in some markets and reduce Coca-Cola system sales. In addition, some of these raw materials, such as aspartame, acesulfame potassium and sucralose, are available from a limited number of suppliers. We cannot assure you that we will be able to maintain favorable arrangements and relationships with these suppliers. An increase in the cost or a sustained interruption in the supply or shortage of some of these raw materials that may be caused by a deterioration of our relationships with suppliers or by events such as natural disasters, power outages, labor strikes or the like, could negatively impact our net revenues and profits (p. 15) listed briefly, but there is no discussion of these risks. Additionally, some risks catalogued by the directors are highly generic. For example, risks arising from 'actions by competitors' or 'government policy changes' will apply to most companies in most industrial sectors. The risk information has not been situated in an industry or company-specific context and this does not help the reader to better understand how these risks may impinge upon the company.

There is a little more risk discussion in Example 2 and some limited contextualisation of the risks. This makes the discussion a little more helpful to the reader, although it is still a very restricted discussion. The company states that the 'businesses have a long record of increasing sales and profits through a combination of investing in modern efficient factories, developing a range of quality products and making sound acquisitions' (Carrs Milling Industries, 2006, p. 10) but this does not explain at all how the risks are being managed or mitigated; rather it is implying that everything will be alright in the future simply because it has been in the past. Thus, it improves on Example 1, but it is still not providing full risk information.

Examples 3 and 4 are more extensive discussions of particular risks that each respective company faces. In discussing the risk mitigation techniques used to address an industry-specific risk in Example 3, the company assists the reader in their assessment of the directors' abilities to proactively manage risk. In its consideration of the risks of potential shortages of raw materials, Example 4 illustrates that companies can be willing to discuss potentially bad risk news and that the discussion can be relatively extensive.

Surveys of UK companies published in 2006 by Deloitte (*Write to Reason*) and PricewaterhouseCoopers (2006) (*Show Me More than the Money*) have also examined narrative discussions within quoted company annual reports. In these surveys disclosures of risks and uncertainties were also found lacking. It was commonplace for the companies to focus on the disclosure of financial risks (for example, interest rate risk and credit risk) and for there to be boilerplate reporting of generalised risks. Relatively few companies were clearly disclosing their principal risks and there was minimal attempt at quantifying risks. These two surveys also confirm the Linsley and Shrives (2006b) and Kajüter (2006) findings that larger companies have a tendency to disclose more risk information. The four examples in Table 9.4 illustrate this phenomenon in an unscientific way. The largest company, Coca-Cola, has wide-ranging risk discussions within its 10-K form. These discussions embrace issues such as risks to product demand originating from health and obesity concerns, uncertainties surrounding future production capacity from potential water shortages and risks to costs caused by packaging legislation. Conversely, the smallest company, Marine Produce Limited, has very limited risk discussions. A positive facet of this is that it does provide the opportunity for smaller companies to learn from larger companies.

Conclusions

Annual reports have been increasing in size, but companies have retained a reluctance to disclose risk information. Given the importance of risk information to investors and other stakeholders it is not unexpected that risk reporting regulations have therefore been brought in by different countries to overcome this inertia. Generally, the risk disclosure regulations are all moving towards the same goal. Namely, they are seeking to have directors provide discussions of the major risks that have impacted upon the company in the past or may impact upon the company in the future. These discussions become most useful for decision-making when they provide an assessment of the size of the impact and when they communicate about company-specific risks and the management of those risks.

This latter point creates a particular dilemma for legislators and regulators. The risks that industry sectors face can differ substantially, and within each industry sector the risks that an individual company may be subject to can diverge greatly. Consequently risk reporting requirements cannot be overly prescriptive. They must allow directors freedom to discuss risks in a manner that is most suitable for that company. However, legislation and regulation that is flexible rather than dogmatic becomes open to interpretation and the eventual outcome may not be as desired. Directors can choose to follow the letter of the law rather than the spirit, and in the case of risk disclosures this may result in the full risk picture remaining unseen.

Organisations such as the AICPA/CMA Canada and the Report Leadership initiative (a group focused on improving corporate reporting) can assist directors through the development of good practice guidelines and the provision of leadership in the area of risk reporting. These may be especially helpful as directors attempt to contend with practical problems such as:

- How to ensure risks are fully discussed, whilst also having a regard for commercial sensitivity?
- How to provide a meaningful assessment of the potential impact (or impacts) that a risk may have?

- How to differentiate between significant and minor risks?
- How to communicate risks so that they will be meaningful to a variety of different stakeholders groups and are not liable to misinterpretation?

Good practice guidelines alone are, however, unlikely to be sufficient. If investors and regulators want directors to engage with the issue of risk communication, then the greatest motivation is likely to come about if directors can be convinced of the benefits associated with risk disclosure. Good risk disclosure requires time and effort, and for directors to fully commit then they need to be certain it is of real value. Investors and other external parties should therefore continue to reiterate the importance of risk disclosures, but credible research that can prove there are gains to be had from improved risk disclosure is more likely to win over directors to the risk reporting cause. If a sufficient number of directors can be convinced that the benefits of risk disclosure outweigh the costs, then a company reporting norm will be established of enhanced risk communication that, in turn, may also encourage some directors to experiment with real-time risk disclosures and in alternative formats.

References

Accounting Standards Board (2006). *Reporting Statement: Operating and Financial Review*. London.

Beretta, S. and Bozzolan, S. (2004). 'A Framework for the Analysis of Firm Risk Communication', *The International Journal of Accounting*, Vol. 39, No. 3, pp. 265–288.

Botosan, C.A. (1997). 'Disclosure Level and the Cost of Equity Capital', *The Accounting Review*, Vol. 72, No. 3, pp. 323–349.

Canadian Institute of Chartered Accountants (CICA) (2002). *Guidance on the Preparation and Disclosure of the MD&A*. Toronto.

Carrs Milling Industries (2006). *Annual Report*.

Courtnage, S. (1998). 'Financial Reporting of Risk', *Tolley's Practical Audit and Accounting*, Vol. 9, No. 6, pp. 61–63.

Deloitte (2006). *Write to Reason*, Available at http://www.deloitte.com/dtt/cda/doc/content/UK_Audit_Writetoreason_06.pdf.

European Union (2003). Directive 2003/51/EC of the European Parliament and of the Council amending Council Directives 78/660/EEC, 83/349/EEC, 86/635/EEC and 91/674/EEC on the annual and consolidated accounts of certain types of companies, banks and other financial institutions and insurance undertakings, PE-CONS 3611/1/03, Brussels.

European Union (2004). Directive 2004/109/EC of the European Parliament and of the Council amending Council Directives on the harmonisation of transparency requirements in relation to information about issuers whose securities are admitted to trading on a regulated market and amending Directive 2001/34/EC.

German Accounting Standards Board (2001). German Accounting Standard No. 5 (GAS 5), *Risk Reporting*, Berlin, Germany.

Hail, L. (2002). 'The Impact of Voluntary Corporate Disclosures on the *Ex-Ante* Cost of Capital for Swiss Firms', *European Accounting Review*, Vol. 11, No. 2, pp. 741–773.

Institut der Wirtschaftsprüfer (IDW) (1998). 'IDW Rechnungslegungsstandard: Aufstellung des Lageberichts (IDW RS HFA 1)', *Die Wirtschaftsprüfung*, Vol. 51, No. 15, pp. 653–662 (in German).

Institute of Chartered Accountants in England and Wales (ICAEW) (1998). *Financial Reporting of Risk – Proposals for a Statement of Business Risk*. London.

Institute of Chartered Accountants in England and Wales (ICAEW) (1999). *No Surprises: The Case for Better Risk Reporting*. London.

Institute of Chartered Accountants in England and Wales (ICAEW) (2002). *No Surprises: Working for Better Risk Reporting*, Briefing 06.02. London.

International Accounting Standards Board (IASB) (2005). *Management Commentary – Discussion Paper*. London.

Kajüter, P. (2001). 'Risikoberichterstattung: Empirische Befunde und der Entwurf des DRS 5', *Der Betrieb*, Vol. 54, pp. 105–111 (in German).

Kajüter, P. (2006). Risk disclosures of listed firms in Germany: A longitudinal study, Paper presented at the Tenth Financial Reporting & Business Communication Conference, Cardiff.

Lajili, K. and Zéghal, D. (2005). 'A Content Analysis of Risk Management Disclosures in Canadian Annual Reports', *Canadian Journal of Administrative Sciences*, Vol. 22, No. 2, pp.125–142.

Linsley, P.M. and Shrives, P.J. (2000). 'Risk Management and Reporting Risk in the UK', *The Journal of Risk*, Vol. 3, No. 1, pp. 115–129.

Linsley, P.M. and Shrives, P.J. (2006a). 'Risk Disclosure: An Exploratory Study of UK and Canadian Banks', *Journal of Banking Regulation*, Vol. 7, No. 3–4, pp. 268–282.

Linsley, P.M. and Shrives, P.J. (2006b). 'Risk Reporting: A Study of Risk Disclosures in the Annual Reports of UK Companies', *British Accounting Review*, Vol. 38, No. 4, pp. 387–404.

PricewaterhouseCoopers (2006). *Show Me More than the Money*. Available at http://www.ofr.pwc.com/uk/tls/ofr/ofr.nsf/id/TBYE-6VEK2Z?Open&SMSESSION=NO.

Schrand, C.M. and Elliott, J.A. (1998). 'Risk and Financial Reporting: A Summary of the Discussion at the 1997 AAA/FASB Conference', *Accounting Horizons*, Vol. 12, No. 3, 271–282.

Woods, M. and Reber, B. (2003). A comparison of UK and German reporting practice in respect of risk disclosure post GAS 5, Paper presented at the 26th Annual Congress of the European Accounting Association, Seville.

Index